COURAGE TO DREAM

LUCIANO PIMENTEL

Translation: Fernanda Doria Batista

Dowslley
Editora

COURAGE TO DREAM

LUCIANO PIMENTEL

Translation: Fernanda Doria Batista

First Edition
2020
Brazil

Dowslley
Editora

Editorial design and cover art: Lucília Dowslley
Layout: Maristela Meneghetti
Translation and Proofreading: Fernanda Doria Batista

Dados Internacionais de Catalogação na Publicação (CIP)
Lumos Assessoria Editorial
Bibliotecária: Priscila Pena Machado CRB-7/6971

P644   Pimentel, Luciano.
     Courage to dream [recurso eletrônico] / Luciano Pimentel. —
   1. ed. — Rio de Janeiro : Dowslley, 2020.
     Dados eletrônicos (pdf).

      ISBN: 978-65-5854-116-5

      1. Ficção. 2. Literatura brasileira. I. Título.

                   CDD B869.3

Dowslley Editora
Contact: (21) 96714-5001
dowslleyeditora2020@gmail.com

Sumário

D. Melfi
Courage to Dream Foreword

The circumstances that surround us, socially, politically, emotionally and spiritually (but not limited to exclusively those) are the variables, the perceptible, that affect us from before the moment we're born and beyond our material death. Those facts, if you choose to believe in them, are ever-present. They are the smog in the air or the cool ocean breeze. They are the violence in the streets of your youth and the quiet serenity of old age. They are the inner satisfactions at an achievement and the crippling discomfort of a missed opportunity.

The details that furnish our days and depict our nights, that sweeten our afternoons, or characterize our dreams are at once subjective and universal. In Luciano Pimentel's Antonio, or Zica, or Felipe, there is a certain subconscious lightness offered by their struggles. They are unique, singular to the promenade of the Ipanema and the strokes on Pimentel's palette of characters and colour. But they are eternally universal. Antonio's search for movement, and more tellingly, his search for understanding reveal a touch of transcendence from the boy who could be anybody else.

Hanging onto Antonio is easy, like hanging on to the tales of Greek mythology, the story of Odysseus and those beings with two heads and one body, split for eternity by Zeus, destined to search for their other halves. Antonio's journey, however, is not eternal in its mythic construction, but its orbital movement, everlasting.

What Antonio may perceive as *progress* or *upward mobility*, we may understand as man's infinite movement. It's a tradition reaching far into the past and extending into the future. Often in a confused, obscure manner, we cannot determine in which direction we are going. Even though the boy from the favela may consider his journey linear, at that 45-degree angle so thoroughly favoured by the society outside of his youth and fraught with the counterarguments of stagnancy so bestowed on him by his neighbourhood, it's much more cyclical than even Pimentel suggests.

We are slightly pained when Antonio returns to the favela after his first adventure in the heart of the city. But it's the book's ending, and Antonio's perception of "winning" and "losing" that really pain us, but in a comforting way. We have the fortune of seeing through his misconception, his actions are in good faith and he is aware that he is playing a game that does not end. But it's only when Antonio acknowledges that he is riding a cycle of circular and oscillating oblique orbits that he will realize he is both always winning and always losing.

Daniel Melfi

Daniel Melfi is a co-founder and the editor-in-chief of 20 Seconds Magazine, a biannual print publication for experimental music and art. He is also a founding member of Famous Grapes Recordings, the event series, platform and record label focused on the visual and aural articulations of sound and electronic music. After growing up in Canada and living and working in Toronto, Melfi relocated to Europe, where he worked as a freelance journalist covering subcultural musical movements across the continent, for outlets like Telekom Electronic Beats, Mixmag, Zweikommasieben, Borshch and a number of others. Melfi currently lives and works in Berlin.

20Secondsmag.com
Famous-grapes.com
Danielmelfi.com

Chapter 1

A Beautiful Place

How am I going to get out of here?

Antonio raised his sleepy eyes to the misaligned roofs of the houses of the *favela*. The sun had just come up, maybe lazy too, but flooding everything with its light.

Who knows the favela was more beautiful at night because the darkness hid the ugliness of unfinished houses and their clay bricks wherever you looked? Unfinished and misaligned, many houses seemed to defy the laws of gravity and rely only on divine goodness to stand. On the streets, countless tangled energy wires hanging from poles made everything ugly, confusing, weird. Garbage bags and dirt scattered all over the streets and alleys.

At night, only the lights of the houses could be seen. At the distance, they looked like a soap opera or movie scene, where everything seems very different, organized and even cute. In broad daylight, in real life, it was quite different...

But the sky was blue. It was so deep and immense, that in his head, the boy found himself wondering if beautiful places, with big green trees, where everything was clean and organized, where houses were colorful and tidy as they showed in cartoons and soap operas really existed or if that was all make believe. But what if it was not? What if there really were places like that?

And even if that were make-believe, it would be great to live in a place like that, even if only for one day.

That March morning, at the age of 12, he swore that if that place existed, he would find it. He was going to get out of the favela. Where to? He did not know yet. How? Not at clue.

But the decision was made. The year was 1991.

Chapter 2

Life is just like this

The work was exhausting. Many hours standing on a busy kitchen. At the end of the day, the price to pay was the throbbing of his feet. But at least he would get a burger, fries and soda on each shift and the salary would pay for a small room.

My hand!

A distraction was enough for the unwanted encounter of his skin and the grill plate to happen.

Antonio was taken to the back room by the manager on duty. There was some burn ointment in the first aid kit. As he put the ointment on his hand, he consoled himself thinking that, at least, he would be a few minutes away from the inhuman kitchen heat, the ubiquitous smell of fried food and the never ending oil that sticks everywhere. He could also sit down for a while, which was good, and his legs appreciated it.

That afternoon, Antonio was lost in his thoughts, dreaming of what his future room would be like, with a bed of his own and a wardrobe, maybe a TV. A TV? Really? He could not tell.

Anyway, it would be a lot better than sleeping on the living room couch and having to store his clothes in the three drawers of the living room rack. There was only one bedroom in his house where his mother and grandmother slept. The idea of finally having a bedroom of his own and being able to leave the favela occupied all his thoughts ever since that morning almost two years before.

However, time was slow, as usually occurs when we really want something to happen soon. When we count the days for something to happen, they insist on dragging. Minutes become hours, hours become days and one day seems to take a whole year to pass! Too bad this never happened at school during breaktime or on lunch breaks at work! Time seems to choose when to drag and when to fly.

Antonio had created a place in his mind and while orders were placed non-stop and the grill plate turned into a sea of patties, oil and smoke, he ran away to the image of himself, deep blue skies on a sunny day, walking down a clean street, green trees on both sides, beautiful and colorful well finished houses.

But there were obstacles, his age for starters, he was still a minor. Who would rent a room for a fourteen-year-old boy? Then the most serious problem: telling his mother and grandmother he wanted to leave home. How could one do that?

Since he had decided to leave, Antonio had been

keeping everything to himself. He did not tell anyone, except Piquito.

He had the noisy four-year-old cockatiel since he was ten. His uncle Olavo had given it to him for his birthday. Piquito stayed in his cage during the day. At night, Piquito liked to perch on the back of the couch where Antonio slept. It was at bedtime that the boy would tell Piquito about his day, good and bad things, but mostly his plans. He wished Piquito could talk, but the closest to talking he did was whistling the anthem of his uncle's favorite football team whenever somebody shouted "goal". Other than that, he would just sing, followed by his almost inaudible mumbling. Still, the way Piquito sometimes turned its head aside swinging its body between one paw and another gave the impression that the bird could listen and understand everything Antonio was talking about.

Not that he did not share his thoughts with his mother and grandmother, but Antonio hardly saw his mother during the week. Irene had two jobs so she could pay the bills. When she arrived home, he would be asleep and when he woke up to go to school, she would already be gone to work. They had moved into their grandmother's house after José, his grandfather, died, about seven years before. Not having to pay rent anymore would be a relief for Irene. Maria lived off the pension left by José. Her daily activities were basically embroidering, cooking, and praying. Antonio was more than her grandson; he was like a son to her. A boy who knew nothing about life and still had a lot to learn.

Could he leave them?

Living with them was great. He never lacked the affection of his mother or his grandmother's love, neither did he lack being smacked with a slipper by the old lady when he misbehaved, like when he broke the house gate pretending to be climbing Everest. Everything was going well until the gate could not bear the boy's euphoria shaking the bars and fell to the ground in a tremendous bang. The old woman almost had a heart attack. It was lunchtime, when Maria heard the noise, she ran from the kitchen so stunned that she forgot the pot in which she was frying some garlic. She only realized when she felt the smell of burning garlic and saw the smoke coming out of the house. That smacking was deserved, as so many others were too.

The problem of the favela was that to get to his house there were the surroundings that turned his stomach and saddened him. Not long before, there had been a shooting and a man died. His body was lying on street Antonio used to take on his way back from school. Someone had covered the body with a white sheet, but the blood that stained the sheet also flowed through the asphalt. Certain horrors cannot be disguised. Wide-eyed, Antonio walked by the body and, call it bad luck for the boy and amusement for some of the curious people who accompanied everything from their windows, a gust of wind lifted the tip of the sheet knocking down the candle that had been lit for the soul of the deceased and showed his face. Antonio's legs faltered and his heart froze in his chest. A scream of horror arose shaking his entire body, desperation took over and he only stopped running when he was home. That image never left his head.

They had to leave that place. But how would they do that? What about his mother? What about his grandmother? Maria would never leave the house that José built with so much sacrifice. His mother would not leave his grandmother alone at all. They both had their differences, but love was much bigger. There were many things to figure out, and his finals were coming up. That would take a lot of work. Maybe he should give up and leave things the way they were. Maybe that is just how life really is…

Chapter 3

Candy, jellybeans, stove lighters

Today was the big day! Nothing else mattered.

Finally, after an endless thirty days, the reward for so much sweat, burns, frying and tears came. Of course, he had not figured out how to rent a room at his age or how to tell his mother and grandmother that he had decided to leave the house yet.

In fact, Antonio had no idea how to solve these problems. The night before, he had watched a movie on TV in which a 12-year-old boy made a wish on a shooting star that the next day he woke up at the age of twenty-eight. It might as well happen to him. When he went to bed, he looked at Piquito, who was already nestled in his usual place on the back of the couch.

"Think about about it, Piquito! I wake up tomorrow at 28 years old already inside my new room with everything fixed! I will make you a really nice little perch on the side of my bed and everything will be all right." Piquito, who was almost falling asleep, turned his head sideways and grumbled, turning its eyes upwards. Who said animals are not wise?

The next morning, Antonio was still fourteen and real life called him in his grandmother's voice for coffee.

"Wake up! Coffee is ready. Do you want some milk? I do. I made yellow couscous. Hmmm!"

The train was, as usual, crowded. Antonio preferred the bus, but his grandmother had heard on the radio that an accident between a truck and a van had closed President Vargas Avenue near the Sambadrome and traffic was stopped since Leopoldina Avenue. He did not want to be late, especially on the day of his first payment.

"Candy, jellybeans, stove lighters!" one of those so common illegal train sellers shouted as he tried to make way among the passengers.
"Can't you see that there is no way you can pass? This isn't the time to sell such things!"
"Ma'am, everyone needs to work. Here are some jellybeans to make your morning sweeter. On the house."
"Oh, give me a break!"

Some passengers laughed while others were indifferent, thinking of their own problems. Antonio laughed as he looked at the silhouette of the Corcovado, firmly holding on to the open door of the train so as not to fall.

He was next in line to get paid. Only one thing seemed strange; most of his colleagues ahead of him in line had the same expression: curved shoulders, low heads, and sad eyes. Some grasped the small white envelope in closed hands so tightly that Antonio could not tell if it was anger or fear.

It could not be anger. Who would be angry about getting paid? It must have been fear. Fear of losing the money. Antonio knew that feeling quite well. Whenever his grandmother asked him to go out and to buy some bread, she always strongly warned him to walk with tightly closed hands so that when he gave the money to Mr. Nestor it was all sweaty and crushed.

But not all the strength nor care in this world can stop things from happening when they must. Until today he does not know where the two Reais went to. He was supposed to use that money to buy sugar for his grandma's birthday cake. They disappeared. They were just gone. He was sure he had them in his hands until at least the last corner before the store. He took the sugar packet and when it was time to pay, where was it? He looked everywhere for what seemed to be forever. He retraced his steps and nothing. Sugar free cake and a smacking.

The last colleague rushed out of the office hurriedly putting the envelope in his pocket. Antonio seemed to be one of the few to have a half-smile on. Deep down, he was very excited and eagerly waiting for his turn, but given the situation, he thought it was best to disguise the excitement.

"Congratulations, young man! You worked very well. Keep it up and one day you might be one of the auxiliary managers of some branch!" said the manager on duty, as he delivered the same white envelope to the boy. Encouraged by the man's words, Antonio opened a broad smile raising his thick eyebrows and said:

> *"Thank you very much!"*
> *"Don't spend all your pay on candy and stickers, huh!"*
> *"I don't like candy. I'm going to rent a room just for myself with that money,"* he answered triumphantly.
> *"A room? With that money?"* the man asked surprisedly.
> *"Yes. With a bed, a wardrobe and maybe a TV!"*
> *"Son, you can do a lot of things with that money, but it's not enough to rent a room. If you use all your money to pay for the room, how will you eat? There's food to buy, too. It's not enough. Have you thought about it?"*

No. Antonio had not thought about the food. He had spent the last thirty days making his plans and, in his head, everything was right: the bed, the wardrobe, the TV... He had not considered food... in fact, it had only occurred to him at that moment. He never cared about food, because all he had to do was to go to the table whenever his grandmother called him to eat, and there was the food. Even with difficulties, his mother could provide. He could not cook either. His plan had serious flaws.

The return home that day was sad and full of thoughts. There was a new feeling. If he earned more, there would be no problem. But he did not.

At that moment he understood the look in his colleagues' eyes earlier. Yes, you can feel angry when you get paid. Also, the fear of losing the little that is received. Antonio already knew fear. But anger was something new to him.

"Candy, jellybeans, stove lighters!" Shouted the seller trying to make way among the passengers. *"Jellybeans to make your night sweeter".*

Chapter 4

It is what it is

"Leaving the favela? Renting a room? Have you gone crazy?" Her loud laughter made the precarious floor made boards in the shack quake. And the more she repeated the questions, the louder and shriller Zica laughed.

"Can you not laugh, please? This way the whole favela will know it!"! – asked Antonio.

Useless. The more Zica laughed, the more she felt like laughing. It was like when we are laughing at a joke and we enter an infinite loop where our own laughter is why we are laughing, and we do not even know the why we are laughing anymore. Antonio frowned and turned his back to leave.

> *"Wait!" Zica shouted as she wiped her eyes with black fat hands. "Are you serious?"*
> *"Yes."*
> *"But why? Don't you love your mother and grandmother?"*
> *"Of course, I do! It has nothing to do with them. It's about this place. It's ugly, it's dirty, it doesn't have trees, there's no green, there are shootings, the open-air sewage smell everywhere, there are junkies, garbage, screaming, rats. It's scary."*

"Calm down. You're angry. That's it, that's all. This shall pass."

"You don't understand. Haven't you ever wanted to leave?"

"Getting out of here? Where to?"

"Anywhere! A beautiful place, with green, beautiful houses. Somewhere clean..."

"I like it here. I was born and raised here. That's all I know. When I want to see something beautiful, I turn the TV on and watch a movie, a soap opera. They always make movies in beautiful places. The soap operas, too. The rich have big houses with beautiful pools and gardens. As I watch it, it feels like I live there and I'm rich too. That's fine with me. Also, I could never make it out of here. You must have a lot of money to rent something out of the favela. The cleaning services that I do with my mother are just enough to pay the bills and a little for me to do my hair and nails on the weekend. We also have the dance funk parties. You're a fool. You don't know what you're going to miss. I'm not going anywhere."

"But wouldn't you like to have a big house with a pool and a garden?"

"Listen: that's life. There are the rich and the poor. Each person belongs to their own place. We were born poor. We belong here. If you were to be born rich, you would have. Trying

to change the course of life will only bring you a headache and sadness. It is what it is."

"You don't understand. I can't live here. Every day is agony when I must leave home and face the street, go past the trash or throw myself on the ground when there's a shooting, I can't take it anymore! I don't feel like I belong here, I want to see beautiful things that aren't just on TV or in the movies. I want to live, I want to feel it, I want to see it with my eyes."

"Nice speech. But face it. Don't be selfish! You're only thinking of yourself. Who do you think you are, Antonio? You're poor. You're son and grandson of poor people. You work in the kitchen of a fast-food restaurant. You're lucky you like to study and live with those books you read. I don' know how you can do it. That must be it. You think too much, you read too much. And that makes you think you are better than others, you know more than others and that you are too good to live here. It's hurting you. Soon you'll start talking about going abroad. Your father was a cook in a ship, right? He traveled the world. You told me that story."

"And that's what she said, Piquito. She said I act all high and mighty and I wanted to be better than everyone else. She said I read and think too much, that I was selfish and all I could think about was myself. And I thought she was going support me and even help me with mom and

grandma. Quite the opposite. What's wrong with wishing more? Why did she call me selfish just because I want to be somewhere better?"

Piquito, as the good friend he was, moved and pecked on Antonio's head as if looking for something on his hair. Maybe it was his way of comforting the boy since he had no hands to show affection. Antonio could not sleep. Suddenly, he was in front of a very large and beautiful house with high iron gates. He wanted to come inside, but it was closed. He could see a garden in the back. He started digging the earth with his own hands to try to pass under the gate. He heard laughter in the distance. He felt a hand on his shoulder. It was Zica. She was carrying a folded white sheet in her other hand, still stained with blood.

Chapter 5

Hot Dog

The steam rising from the soft asphalt made everything dance in the background. Cars, legs, paws and poles. The hot wind, which sometimes blew, brought no relief. It was another Summer day in Rio. But Antonio would not go to beach that day.

"Hot dog and juice for 1 Real!" Zica shouted in her powerful voice.

She would invite the costumers and prepare the sandwiches, while Antonio handled the juice and the change. At the end of the day they put the booth down and Antonio carried everything to the shed where they kept the material. It had only been two weeks since they started the business. *"We won't make money working for somebody else, Antonio. We set up this booth, in a little while we'll have a second one, a third... There is also the coconut water business. I know a guy who started with one booth and now he's got about ten sales points on the beach. You have to save some money if you really want to leave the favela."*

Antonio divided his day between the restaurant kitchen in the morning, then he worked with Zica until about six o'clock in the afternoon, after taking everything to a shed, he would go to school in the evening. He studied in the evening now, as it was common for high schoolers in Brazil when they had to work. He liked the movement of the street, the passersby, the excitement of the cars, the executives in suits and ties, the beautiful girls who balanced their nice legs on their high heels through the Portuguese stone streets of Largo da Carioca. He just could not stand the heat… and the pigeons. He hated them both. "Pigeons are like rats," his mother used to say. He was afraid of rats. So, the combination of rats and wings made pigeons look worse than they were.

But it was not long before the day was over. And on Saturdays, there were the English lessons. His mother's idea. When she was single, she had taken some English lessons until she could not afford the monthly fee anymore. The books remained though, and the curious Antonio tried to read them asking questions she could no longer answer.

"Use this money you get at the restaurant to take English lessons. You like it, son. English is spoken all over the world and it can open many doors. I wish I could have continued studying" she said.

Between one client and another, he was trying to do his English homework, it was already past its deadline. He had to do exercises on his workbook and answer a questionnaire. The week had been tight, but fortunately the hot dog booth was beginning to form a clientele. It could have been some spell that Zica put in the hot dog sauce with the bacon. She cooked well. "Hunger doesn't start in the belly. Hunger starts in the nose," she said. "You fry the garlic, because no one resists fried garlic smell, then cover it with the bacon. The smell goes around the block" and she laughed with her hand on the fat waist. "Take a good look at me, I know what I'm talking about. We are what we eat. That's why I'm like this," she tapped her round belly, "delicious." Both laughed. They made jokes about the passersby and made up stories. "That one has got wet hair at lunchtime, humm. That other one walks a little weird…" that way the afternoon went on, and they made a living.

"A hot dog, please." Asked a girl with a clipboard on her hands.

"Sure thing! Here or bag?" Antonio hurried to talk to her. She must have been about sixteen, like him. She was white with sweet honey eyes and black hair. Long and wavy.

"Here," she answered with a smile. She had a nice smile too. He always liked wide and beautiful smiles with big, long teeth. Maybe because it reminded him of his mother's smile, which he hardly ever saw, or maybe because when a person with teeth like that smiles, it feels like they are hugging everyone with the size of their smile. People with beautiful teeth have an obligation to smile

and captivate others with the beauty of their smile.

"There you go. Cashew or passion fruit?"

"Cashew."

"Hot today, huh?" He rehearsed a conversation.

"Yes. So hot, and so far, I haven't sold anything."

"What do you sell?"

"I sell theater tickets. You can buy spare tickets for shows or subscribe to the magazine and receive a monthly discount on tickets. But nowadays nobody cares about theater, culture or anything. People are short on money. No one has time for anything in the city center. They don't even stop to listen to me. Some people think it's a scam."

"I know it. Sometimes, when things are slow here, we set the booth up at Treze de Maio Street to see if things get better."

And that's when Antonio had an idea, which would be fantastic if it worked! It would be a win-win. His English teacher, the theater girl, the cultural establishments of the city and Antonio, who already saw himself spending more time in the company of that smile.

Chapter 6

Copacabana Beach

They had already sold more than half of Maria Clara's monthly quota after three hours. The idea was simple, but ingenious. Antonio translated almost all the questions that Maria Clara used when she approached someone to English – of course he needed the help of a dictionary. He did not know some of the words in English, for those they relied on mimics. As for the translation, he handed it over to the English teacher to get extra credit to compensate for the homework he had not done before, he wanted to apologize.

They met in front of the Copacabana Palace, one of the most famous and bustling hotels in the city at around 1pm, because he had to go to the English class and Maria Clara lived far away and could not get there earlier.

She was so pretty. She wore shorts, sandals, and a spaghetti strap top. He could not take his eyes off that strap that insisted on falling off her shoulder. She wore her hair up on a ponytail and some of it was loose on the back of her neck. A pair of sunglasses completed her look.

Maria Clara waved to invite the passing tourists and Antonio started the conversation in English. Perhaps it was curiosity, pity, or for fun, but most tourists would stop and listen to what he was trying to say in his very thick English. He wanted to talk more, however, he did not master the language and could not say more than the lines he had memorized from his script.

Germans, Americans, a Russian woman in a pink dress and a red feathered hat. People could be so different! Were there favelas in Germany? Or in France? No. They must be very nice and chic places. Those tourists must have been very rich to fly and visit Rio. He would like to see those places. To see what it was like. He did not even have to live there, for him, just being able to know the place would be enough. The ideal place to live would be out of the favela, with some green: a garden, a tree, anything. But what if... These thoughts came in waves that afternoon, but the "what if..." became a fixed idea.

They had a lot of fun. In the end of afternoon, tired, Maria Clara said: *"Let's have some coconut water?"* *"Hey, 'yes', I mean, 'sim'. That's a great idea."* He answered with a smile, confusing English and Portuguese. *"I know a place. Where do you live?"* She wanted to know.

He knew that sooner or later that subject would come up. He wished he could avoid that moment for as long as possible. Once he mentioned that he lived in a favela, she would certainly never look at him again. It would be over. He tried to dodge the question.

"You don't know the neighbourhood..." he replied as he tried to buy some time. But as the silence was getting more and more awkward, he had no choice, but to answer her.

"I live in Penha." He lied saying he lived in a nice district of Rio.

He did not have the guts to tell the truth. Everything was going so well that he was afraid to spoil it. When would a pretty girl like that agree to go out with a slum dweller like him? Everything was great, but the place you live matters, and it would become a problem. He was ashamed of where he lived. It was not his fault he lived there; he knew that. But still, he was ashamed. What would the others think? It was like having a sticker on your forehead: "slum dweller". People looked at you differently. Maybe one day the favela would be in and people would even think the idea of "community" to be a nice one, but that day had not come yet. Working at a restaurant and selling hot dogs on the street was not the best first impression, he still had to live in the favela...

"What about you?" He asked.
"I live in the Acari Favela" Maria Clara replied humbly. The boy's eyebrows rose unconsciously in amazement. He expected everything from her, except that. He thought she would say Tijuca, Méier, Jacarepaguá, once she said she lived far away, but Maria

Clara answered his question so naturally that it was like a slap in Antonio's face. Why did he have to lie? And now how was he going to fix things? *"A lie has short legs, Antonio"* that was what his grandmother would say now. *"Sooner or later, the truth always comes out."* A chill ran through his spine. Why was he such a coward? What now?

"Is that a problem?" She asked.

"Of course not!" He answered with a half-smile.

"You seemed amazed."

"No. I've already been to a favela. I know people who live in favelas." What was he doing? He could not understand it. He had just lied and now he was making it worse? Why was he doing that? He could feel his stomach turning. He wanted to run away and never see Maria Clara again. Liar. Coward. That was all he could think.

"Cool." She said.

"Yeah... Look! The sun is setting!" He said as he pointed at the sun trying to change the subject.

The sun was going down behind the Dois Irmãos Mountain, in Leblon, painting the blue sky with orange and reddish tones. From the stones of the Arpoador you could see people walking by the beach or watching the sunset as they clapped. It was summer. It was Rio. It was the beauty of the sunset hugging everyone with no distinction. It was the smell of the ocean that filled up the air as the strong waves met the fine sands of the beach and deeply penetrated in peoples' nostrils, wrapping everything around it. The taste of salt becoming sweet on the thin and soft lips of Maria Clara. Maria Clara and her beautiful smile that hugged Antonio.

And at that moment nothing else mattered. It was Antonio's first kiss and he struggled to do the best he could. He reached the back of Maria Clara's neck and undid her hair. Her hair tangled in his hands, his fingers playing with her hair. The other hand gently touched her soft and warm face. He gave small kisses, alternating with long and intense ones, with tongues and bites. His heart was pounding, and it felt like it was about to explode. He felt it down his spine, it took over his body. His feet and hands were tingling and his muscles so stiff. Butterflies in his stomach, as if he were on a roller coaster. He took deep breaths between one kiss and another. Touching hands, dark skins, white skins. Fever...

He was under her, so he would not hurt Maria Clara's back. He did not care about the rocks scratching his back. Black hair like a waterfall all over his chest. The waves hit the rocks and water splashed all over their bodies. Their sound covering up groans and whispers. He did not know what to do or how to do it until Maria Clara's soft hand showed the way inside her. It was ecstasy. It was summer. It was Rio.

Chapter 7

Cocada

What was the address again? Alfandega Street with Rio Branco Street? Paulo's handwriting was hard to read. He should have been a doctor instead of a lawyer. No, it was 10 Assembleia Street. He was far. Walking would be faster, traffic was jammed. The second to last floor belonged to a law firm. He carried documents that needed to be signed. Then, he had to notarize them and go straight to Barra. And then, finally, he had to go back to the office in Cinelândia. Not before having something to eat, it was already three in the afternoon and he had not eaten anything. The elevator doors opened, and Antonio forgot what he was thinking about when he encountered one of the most beautiful views of the Guanabara Bay that he had ever seen. The number 10 on Assembleia Street was called Candido Mendes Building and it was one of the three tallest buildings in the city. It opened in 1978, from the top of its forty-nine floors, you could see the entire city. Where Antonio was, he could see the Rio-Niteroi Bridge on the left, the city of Niteroi in the background and the ferryboat terminal just ahead. Squinting a little, he could even see the outline of the Teresópolis Ridge and its characteristic peak, the Finger of God. The sunlight reflected on the water of the bay creating bright and indefinite shapes: another bridge, only that it was made of pure light. What a beautiful view! Downstairs people walked hurriedly, making plans, rhythmic. Suddenly, a plane approached to land at the Santos Dumont Airport. He was late, but work could wait a while. He wanted to see it landing. The plane was fast approaching, floating, it was already close to the ground, but he could not see the landing because of other buildings. What a shame. It must be nice to fly. Would he ever fly? Who knew what else life held?

Two years before he could hardly imagine that selling theater tickets to tourists at the beach would have been such a good idea. It was on one of those Saturdays that he met Paulo. The lawyer was a long-time resident of that area and used to walk his dog on the boardwalk in the late afternoon, when the sun was weaker. In one of those days, the dog escaped his lash and ran aimlessly. All those pints at the Pavão Bar accumulated around Paulo's belly and contributed to the dog's great escape, making it hard for Paulo to keep up. Antonio heard the fuss and cornered the small poodle between a kiosk and a stone bank. Paulo still on the run, panting, waved as he thanked the boy. Eventually, the boy would be friends with Cocada, who always greeted him on his walks, as well as with Paulo…

"I won't be able to walk Cocada next Saturday. Would you like to walk him? I'll pay."
"Sure thing! Thank you very much."

Paulo trusted Antonio more and more, until one

day, he offered Antonio office boy position in this firm. It was a formal job. Monday to Friday, from 8 to 6, they would give him transportation vouchers and food stamps. The boy accepted it, but he would have to quit his job in the restaurant first. Then he had to tell Zica that he could not sell hot dogs with her anymore.

It was easy in the restaurant. He thanked the manager for the opportunity and his colleagues all pinched in for one last meal with a double burger and a big ice cream.

His talk with Zica was weird, though. In fact, since he had met Maria Clara, Zica was different with him. They still joked around, but she seemed angrier than usual. Ok, Zica was not the most stable person he knew. He even risked messing with her: "Maria Zuleide dos Santos" She would lose it and call him names. She hated being called by her name. She preferred Zica.

There were days she would say: *"Don't mess with me, I'm not in a good mood today."* And she spent the rest of the afternoon quiet. When he asked what was wrong, she would say it was the heat, or the lack of money or a new diet that made her hungry and impatient. Hard to know what was really wrong with her.

When he told her, he had broken up with Maria

Clara, she did not say a word. It was one of the few times he saw her quiet like that.

Maria Clara's family was from São Paulo and her father, a welder, had gotten a job at an automaker in the ABC region, so they were going back to São Paulo. They were going to stay with relatives until everything was settled. Well, that was the story she had told him.

They had not been together that long. Just a couple of months: eight Saturdays. After selling tickets, they drank coconut water and made out. Those had been the best Saturday afternoons that Antonio had ever had in his life. The last time they met, Maria Clara promised she would write to him and asked for his address. The lie had taken its toll. But Antonio still was not able to tell the truth. He gave her his real address, however, but he said his district was Penha.

He had never been able to tell Maria Clara the truth. Would she suspect him? Was she lying too when she said she was moving out, exactly because she suspected he was lying? He liked her and she seemed to like him too. The only problem was that he had screwed up right from the start with that lie. The guilt, the shame of where he lived, those feelings consumed him. And he did not know how to get rid of them unless he told the truth. But he could not. The way Maria Clara said she lived in the favela, so naturally, seemed throw a spotlight on his cowardice. They say we lie about things we would like to be true. He would very much like his lie to be true. Besides, everyone lies, has lied, or will lie at some point in life. It is proven. The point was that a lie was a sign of weakness. And it bothered him.

Deep down he was even relieved at the end. The happiness he felt when they met was constantly accompanied by the anguish his lie caused him. He played a role all the time and felt bad about it. On the other hand, he could not find the courage to tell her the truth. Not even Piquito knew it.

Meeting Paulo was one of the best things that could have happened. He had a big library and did not mind lending his books or answering Antonio's questions.

Antonio's reading habits had been cultivated very early, thanks to his very religious grandmother who taught him the first letters with the Bible. His first book: The Book of Genesis. Antonio did not understand much of it. And at the same time he was terrified of the devil, he felt sorry for him. In his childish innocence, he asked God to forgive the devil and end hell. That way, everyone would be happy. Until the day his grandmother heard one of his prayers and explained that was not possible because there was no forgiveness for what the devil had done. Antonio did not understand how God could not forgive the devil because, by experience, even if he made the worst mess possible, his mother would scold him, but she would forgive him eventually. How could God be so loving and not forgive? It had been a long time since the devil had made his mess. Good for him that his mother, who after a few kisses and apologies, would hug him and offer something tasty to eat.

In the end, when he went to the pre-school, at the age of five, he could read, write his own name, and do a little math. He also knew the names of all the books in the Old Testament by heart.

Paulo was very cultured. He loved the history and voice of Luciano Pavarotti. Whenever he was in town, he would teach Antonio all about it. He traveled around the country for work and when he came back, he always went to the office at least three times a week. At the end of the day, between one glass of whiskey and another, he would tell Antonio about his trips: the food, the hotels, art and poetry. He reflected on life and its meaning.

Antonio would listen to everything dazzled by the eloquence of Paulo. In his head he imagined himself inside a plane, traveling the country, with many stories and adventures to tell, bringing souvenirs from each place, just as the lawyer.

> *"Study, Antonio. I wasn't born with a silver spoon in my mouth either. It took a lot of sacrifice for me to go to college. We plant the*

seed first and then take care of the plant. We patiently water it every day. Until it turns into a tree, providing us fruits and shade. But it all starts with a seed. Look, it doesn't matter where we start, what matters is the destination. Don't ever forget that."

He recited phrases from great philosophers such as Aristotle: *"Culture is the best comfort for old age."* Sometimes, inspired by the whiskey, he declaimed in Latin: *"suae quisque fortuna faber est."* Man makes his own destiny.

Even today he could clearly remember his words:

"No one can take knowledge away from you. Once you get it, no one can steal it. Knowledge is freedom from all ignorance... There's no prison worse than that."

Antonio always nodded. For him, his prison was the favela. He felt like his chest was being crushed when he went home. Especially when he had to deliver documents at the rich parts of the city. The streets were so clean with beautiful trees. He entered beautiful houses that smelled so good, with their gardens and swimming pools. That was exactly how Zica talked about soap operas. When he was waiting for the clients with the documents, he imagined himself living in such places and the reality of the favela seemed distant and blurry. He felt rich and happy even if it was for a few hours.

On the other side of the room, Paulo turned the LP record, as he asked:

"What is your biggest dream, young man? Do you already have one?"

Looking through the window, a little bird bathed in a puddle, Antonio answered as if he thought out loud.

"Getting out of the favela. Being able to live somewhere beautiful and traveling by plane, at least once in my life."

He sighed with deeply wet eyes. The knot hurt his throat because of the force he made not to show the waver in his voice, while blinking quickly to hold back the tears.

The needle of record player stopped in the air for a moment. It seemed to weigh and measure each word. Then it went down.

"Vento, vento portami via con té..."

Chapter 8

Suae quisque fortuna faber est

A few months had passed after that afternoon when Paulo called Antonio in his office. Without much ado, Paulo was blunt, as usual.

"A friend of mine has a room to rent in his apartment. He asked me if I knew anyone. I told him about you. Is your dream still on?"

"Yes!" He answered astonished, mouth half open. The yes came before he could think of it. He had waited so long to say that yes that it exploded out of his lungs... With his eyes fixed on the lawyer, he could not identify what he was feeling. It was like receiving an electrical discharge on his body. He could not believe what was happening! Six years had gone since he decided he was going to leave the favela. The reality of the misery, poverty, and violence he saw every day gradually undermined his resistance, imposing its law, its fatality. It had been stealing his hope of better days, robbing his smile. He had felt his revolt escalating, squeezing his chains: a prisoner of his own house, hostage of life. All the times he had been late for work because he had to wait for a shooting to stop so he could get out of the house. How many things had he lost to the

flooded open-air sewage river near his house when it rained a lot? And now this? Did his grandmother's God really exist? Had it finally looked at him? Was it his turn?

"Great. I don't know how much the rent is. I'm going to talk to him. I'll let you know as soon as I get an answer."

"Thank you very much, Paulo." That was all he could faintly babble. He was baffled. He could not believe his life was really changing for the better. That his dream was finally going to come true. He could feel his heart explode in his chest. His head was spinning. *"Excuse me,"* he asked. When he left the room, he could not say a word. He was more than happy. Suddenly, anything was possible. Everything had changed. Luck had changed!

But... that was when he realized that it also meant that he should tell his mother and grandmother. And suddenly a shadow of fear began to emerge on the horizon of his soul. He was an only child. He had always wanted a brother to play with, but his parents separated when he was very young. His mother never got married again. He was all they had. How would he talk to them? How would he do it? What would he say?

Walking to the bus stop, his mind was in a spin.

How would they react? What if they started crying? He would not resist. He would not have the strength. He could never stand to see a woman crying and when it came to his mother it was something he could not even think about. Both crying would be too much for him. They had always been very close and had gone through so many things together. Even though he did not see his mother much, he knew she loved him more than anything and he loved her. If she worked that hard, it was because they needed it. His grandmother was his second mother. She had taught him right from wrong, helped with homework, taken care of his clothes. And when he was a teenager, she would still ask if he wanted a mug of warm milk at bedtime. He received her blessing and her kiss at bedtime. How could he separate from them? Maybe he was being selfish as Zica had said. He was just thinking of himself. He could not remember where he had heard or read that life was made of choices.

Every choice involved a compromise. And there he was. He should choose. He would have to give up. He could not have both. But it was not fair! Why wasn't he born rich? In another house. Somewhere else. If he had been born rich, he would not have to make that kind of choice of having to decide between his family and his dream of living in a better place. Such cruelty! If only life was different, they would already live in a better place and everything would be different! Everything would be fine!

But no.

They could not afford to live somewhere else. He had not been born rich. He had also just realized that he had reached the end of the line and that he should have gotten off the bus five stops before.

As he walked home, his legs were heavy, his steps dragged and shoulders shrug as if the weight of the world and the responsibility of his life were on his back. And they were.

When he got home, the table was set inviting him to dinner. It was Friday and his mother would be home soon.

"Man makes his own destiny..."

Was that it?

He was not hungry, but he tried to act as natural as possible. His mother told about her day, as usual. Sometimes she was interrupted by his grandmother, who sometimes dropped one of her catchphrases: "God help us all!", when her mother mentioned the milk prices and the bus fare going up.

"Do you know that boy Quico, Zé's son?"

It would be better to wait until after dinner before

saying something. Or now? Maybe tomorrow? Perhaps saying nothing for now seemed reasonable. There was nothing decided yet. Everything could disappear as fast as it appeared and jumping the gun could start an unnecessary crisis. But they might also feel betrayed, because he should have spoken earlier. It might look like he was running away from something. Anyway... so many things could happen, so many possibilities and no decision.

"Antonio, did you hear what I said, honey? Is everything okay? His mother insisted. Her eyes gazing at him and then at Maria, and then at the boy again.

"Oh... Yes, mom. It's all right, I think I remember Quico. What about him?"

"He's in the hospital. A stray bullet hit his leg near the Maracana Stadium.

"What?"

"Dear, God!"

"But is he okay?"

"Yes, thank God. But do you see the irony? A person lives in the favela and is hit by a stray bullet walking out of it. Go figure. May God have mercy on us..." continued his mother cleaning her mouth after another bite in the beautiful liver steak with onions still steaming on the plate.

"God knows all things and things only happen if they are meant to. All we can do is trust and hope for the best" she sighed and started clearing the table.

"More food?"

"No, Grandma, thank you. I'm fine."

Antonio was not there. Well, his body might have been, but his mind wandered around thinking of a million ways to approach the issue with his family and none of his ideas seemed good enough to be put into practice. He had to find the right time. But when would that be? How do you know the right time to do something like that?

"Son, tomorrow is Saturday, but I was asked to take an extra shift in the morning. Do you want to come with me? Do you remember where it is? In the Cinelândia Square."

"Yes, Mom. Sure!" Maybe that was the right time. Was his grandmother really right?

The Passeio Público Park was an oasis in the city center; its huge almond trees with wide trunks and thick canopies and its centenarian palm trees worked the magic. A flock of pionus parrots was making its habitual fuss as they flew from a tree to another, they seemed to be greeting the Wonderful City. As they strolled through the park, Antonio and his mother watched the birds on their way to the Cinelândia Square.

"Watch out, dear!" An apparently dead sparrow

chick on Antonio's way made his mother draw the boy's attention, gently pulling him by the hand.

"I wonder what happened to it." Antonio lamented.

"It has probably fallen off its nest, son." As she answered, they noticed another curious sparrow observing the small bird. "Let's give them some space" said his mother. As both were curious too, they got out of the sparrow's way, but just enough so they could observe both birds. The bird approached the baby bird a little and poked it with its beak. As there was no answer, it flew away. Mother and son continue their path.

"So, what was it you were trying to say yesterday, dear?"

At that very moment, it felt like he was falling, as fast as a stone falling off a high tree. Maybe it took him a little too long to answer.

"What... Mother? No... It was nothing." He looked down hoping that this answer would be enough. Moms are weird. They seem to be able to read thoughts. We do not need to say a word or even to be close to them. It is an instinct like a voice that speaks to and through them.

"You know God gives many people different gifts, don't you? But mothers get a special one, the sixth sense." There! She was reading his thoughts again. He felt like he was shrinking as she was growing bigger and bigger. There was no escape anymore. And that was when he thought, "Why am I running away?" Maybe that was the right moment his grandmother talked about the night before. "Man makes his own destiny." He recalled in Paulo's voice. The cold air slowly penetrated his nostrils, going down his throat, filling his lungs. He closed his eyes. "I want to leave the house, Mom." The words came out with his breath. They came out of his mouth and lungs, his mind and soul. And as they left, Antonio's body was lighter. He could not take that much tension any longer. All those years, months, days, hours. He wanted to get rid of that weight. He could not run away from himself anymore. It was like an unresolved issue that emerges at the most inappropriate occasion making sweet moments taste bitter. Like a reminder of a pending issues that needs to be resolved and that moment can no longer be postponed. And you try to sweep it under the carpet, but then you realize that by doing that you are just postponing the inevitable. And that anguish takes away some colors of the moment. "I once heard that to start a journey, you need to set foot on the road. A long time ago, before I

had you, I wanted to leave home too and have own my life. Times were different for me, as a woman, it was very difficult and not well seen by the society to leave home and be alone. Back then, a successful woman should know how to cook well, get married, have children and a very large house to take care of. It revolted me a lot because that was not how I pictured myself. That worked for my mother, but not for me. I wanted to study to become a doctor and go to Paris…" she smiled, "but I always thought this was just a distant dream. Maybe I was right. Maybe not. But since I've never tried, I'll never know, right?" She pulled Antonio by the chin and looked deep into his damp eyes.
"I will always be your safe haven. I might always live in a simple house, but there will always be a place for you in it, as long as I live, my dear boy. You can dock your little boat here whenever you want. But remember, boats aren't meant to be docked. Try and find out how far you can go."

He could not hold the tears anymore and they rolled free and uncontrolled. Like a dam that opens floodgates to balance the water level. They hugged so hard they felt their hearts beating against each other. They hugged and cried for what felt like forever. It was one of those life changing moments.

"Let's get going, the mall is going to open."

"But what about work?"

"There's no work. I just wanted some time alone with you, son. We hardly see each other during the week, and I know you love McDonalds burgers."

"Cool! Mom! You had it all figured out, didn't you?"

"I'm a mother, boy. God only gives the sixth sense to mothers, remember?" She winked.

"But how do we tell Grandma?"

"Leave your grandmother to me. She is my mother. She too has her sixth sense." She sighed closing her eyes for a second and let a small smile slip.

A few weeks later he was called to Paulo's office at the end of the day.

"Well, boy, you can have the room. I've already spoken to my friend. Is your dream still up?" Paulo got up and headed to his mini bar across the room to pour himself a dose of whiskey. On the other side of the room, Antonio accompanied the lawyer with his eyes, then focusing his gaze on a small statue on the table. An eagle carved in wood opened its wings as if it were flying. Paulo, lightly shaking the glass in his hand, noticed Antonio's look. He saw his internal struggle, the hesitation. Would he take it or not? He remembered when he had made his own choices, one of them was between studying medicine, as his father wanted him to, or going to law school, his passion. After the first sip, he continued.

"This is another lesson in the school of life. When the path is shown to us that is when we exercise our free will to choose whether we will follow it or not. Life invites us to be writers. Whether we are aware of it or not. It provides us with pencils and a blank book and lets us decide what we will write on each page. In the process of writing the book of our life, we realize, if we are attentive, that each scene has endless possibilities of actions and actors. Endless plots can be unfolded, not to mention characters. Every word written in the book of life is the cause and consequence of the previous word and the next." The lawyer raised his eyes to the window. In the distance, the leaves of the neighbor's mango tree danced in the wind.

"Life and writer are one. We learn that when we get here in this world and get out of it, but in this short interval we call life, we forget what really matters."

But those words would not have any effect on the boy at that moment. We only remember life lessons that really matter when life itself teaches us those lessons. By living and making decisions.

"So?" He asked as he came back to the moment.

Yes! Say yes! He heard a voice in the bottom of his soul. He was scared. He knew that would be a life changing moment. But that same voice was soft, a calm whisper that brought him much peace. As his eyes went from the eagle to the lawyer, he noticed the words coming out of his mouth with no effort. In fact, he did not know where they came from until he realized the final vibration of the dying sound in his chest.

"Yes. I'm in."
"I'm happy, Antonio. Many of the things said here today will be forgotten. Those words, so vivid today, will pass and you will not remember them. That's alright. Every word is a seed cast into the soil of our soul and at the right time, it will germinate. And if we cultivate and take care of it, it will grow with the energy we lend it. *'If you have faith the size of a mustard seed...'*"

Antonio remembered the afternoons he spent reading with his grandmother. He knew that passage from the Bible, he heard his grandmother recite it countless times. He also recalled when the science teacher asked them to do an experiment with a bean. Deep down, beans are also a type seed and when you put one on a piece of cotton with proper watering and light, in a few weeks, it begins to sprout. All it took was patience and the right care. He understood what Paulo meant, but he did not really know how words could be like bean sprouts in our minds.

"... you can say to this mountain, 'Move from here to there,' and it will move." Continued Antonio.

"Nothing will be impossible for you." Paulo added.

"So, young man, what I'm telling you this afternoon will remain forgotten over the years, but some of it will stay, and at the right time, if you're are paying attention, you'll understand." He began reciting slowly, inspired:

"It's not for nothing the tear falls
It's not for nothing the smile appears

It's not for nothing the heart feels heavy
It's not for nothing the mind expands

It's not for nothing the dark night gives way to the day
It's not for nothing the light day gives way to night

It's not for nothing the soul suffers
It is not for nothing ecstasy transcends

It's not for nothing there are stones
It's not for nothing there are flowers

It's not for nothing that nothing makes sense now
It's not for nothing it all makes sense tomorrow

It's not for nothing things are the way they are
It's not for nothing life seems to have no meaning
It's not for nothing you look for the reason
It's not for nothing you find what's never been lost.
Nor that you don't understand it now."

His mind was spinning. What is not for nothing? What did that mean? What was the point of so much suffering, so much poverty, for things to be the way they were.

"Why are people born rich or poor?" He wanted to know.

"Antonio, the way we walk the path is more important than where we come from and where we go to. *'All things are ephemeral under the sky'*". That sentence sounded familiar too.

"Remember I said we are given a pencil and a book when we arrive here? Your book can be finely decorated, or it can be just a sketchbook.

The lesson is to write your story with the resources life has given you. Most of the time, we don't remember how many stories we've written or in how many kinds of books. Some are thin, some are thick, some stories are so short that they only take two paragraphs and others are so long that they take several volumes. And all books are important and stored in a library after they're written."

"But don't we ever stop writing? I don't get it!"
"It's not for nothing you don't get it now."

Chapter 9

A ladder to the future

It was raining. It was a fine, lazy rain on a Saturday morning. Antonio was packing, he was lazy too. It was a mixture of emotions. On one hand, he was thrilled by the unknown, a new life that opened up to him. On the other hand, he was afraid. How were things going to be? How would he manage things without the support and care of his mother? What about the milk and cookies, and his grandmother's kiss before bedtime? He had not thought of that. He had not left the house yet, and he already missed them both. It was funny how scared we can become when our dreams are about to come true. It seems that when that is about to happen there is a pause within, one moment of pause, like that deep breath we take before a dive. At that time of his life he did not have many things: a backpack with clothes and two bags with shoes and books. That was all he could take. It is always easier to take things than to leave them behind. Taking things does not require much thought but leaving them does. It requires screening, choices within choices, it involves feelings. And we do not often want to confront our feelings, even though it is necessary, most of the time. With practice, the process becomes simpler, but not necessarily easier. He could not take his guitar. The room was small, and he did not know the routine of the new house. Maybe they did not like music. Maybe they did. Maybe he would be happier there. Maybe not. There were a lot of "maybes" for a Saturday morning. If he were not happy, he could go back home. It was a relief to know his mother and grandmother would always be there. This thought brought a certain comfort to his heart, but also a disturbance: what if they were not? What if something bad happened to them? Stray bullets, shootings or if the river flooded and its sewage water invaded the house and dragged everything, including them? His mind went back and forth in these assumptions for so long and so fast that he did not even realize it was already nine o'clock in the morning and he had not gone downstairs for breakfast. He was not hungry. He was anxious. He was scared. He was hopeful. He was euphoric and sad. His heart was small and shrunk in his chest. It felt like his life was a half-open door, and he could peak on his future, but he was afraid to open it and pass. On the other hand, he did not feel like he was there anymore. It was like an interworld... a threshold... not here, not there. It was the call of life to expand, to grow, to the adventure of living. He could not go back now. He did not fit there anymore. On the other hand, it was very difficult to loosen the rope that held his boat to the safe haven that his family was.

"Honey, haven't you forgotten anything?"

"No, mom. I think it's all here."

"No, it's not." his grandmother shouted from the kitchen. She came with a bag containing cornmeal cake, his favorite, cream biscuits, cooked rice, beans, star fruit and bananas. The bag was heavier than all the other things Antonio was carrying altogether.

"Grandma! You didn't have to!"

"Mom, what's all that? Antonio's not going to disappear. He's going to live in another district, and he will always come and visit us. Right, son?"

"Of course, mom! Definitely."

"It doesn't matter. He's a young man now and he needs to eat and grow strong. I don't have any money, because all my pension goes to meds, as you know, but that's my way of wishing you good luck. Her voice was overcoming with emotion. She used the hem of her apron to wipe away the tears. Her shaky hands trying to hold tight to the fabric. Antonio dropped his bags, let the backpack fall, and ran to his grandmother followed by his mother. It was a three-generation hug, so tight. Their hearts were beating fast, out of step, tears that had been held back, convulsive. The three of them.

Everything was under control until that moment. However, goodbyes can be capricious. There are words not said and emotions held like waters of a river that silently wait for the smallest breach to sneak and gain space until they burst furiously and free following their course.

"Son, this house will always be yours and we will always be here for you. No distance can come between our love. Promise me we'll be in your heart wherever you go. Be a good man, respect both the laws of men and the laws of your heart. Because your heart will always show you the way and you will use reason to choose the best path."

"Sure, mom."

"Life will bring you many challenges. Sometimes you'll win. Others, you'll lose. Sometimes you'll laugh like a crazy man, others, you'll cry. It's okay. Keep moving forward. At the end of the day, everything is a lesson we learn. Be brave. Everything you need is inside you."

At that moment, Piquito started a small fuss, a sign that there was someone at the gate.

"What's going on, guys? Is everything all right? Oh, my God. Who died? I'm nervous already! Why are you crying?"
"It's nothing, Zica. We're saying goodbye to Antonio. He's leaving."
"Guys! You scared the heck of me! I thought someone had died in yesterday's shooting." And she continued. "It'll be okay. He's moving to Méier, it's so close and he'll visit us. Don't

be like that, be careful with the blood pressure. I need some water, you scared me!" She said shaking her hands, gasping. "No, I need something stronger? Do you have any beer, grandma?" She asked, laughing and making the environment lighter, as she always did.

"You know I don't drink, Zica."

"I know it, grandma! I'm messing with you."

"Well, guys, I have to go now."

"Aren't you staying for lunch?" His grandmother asked, trying to delay his departure.

"It's not going to work, mom. He'd better go before the rain starts to pour. You know buses take forever to come when it's raining."

"I'll go to the bus stop with him." Zica said.

"Good idea, dear! Go with him."

Zica could not have arrived at a better time. She had this way of making fun of things, it was contagious. It was very difficult be sad around her. Her company on the way to the bus stop came at a good time.

As they walked, Antonio observed the poor wooden houses, that entire scenario so familiar to him. He looked back at his house... His mother and grandmother were still at the gate. He waved once more and decided not to look back again.

"You're coming to visit us, right, dude?"

"Of course. Are you crazy? Of course, I am."

"Don't you dare disappear, or I will find you and make one of my scandals in front of your building! You know me. When I'm mad, I'm a force of nature!"

They both laughed. They could see Antonio's bus on the distance.

"Take care, my friend. Follow your path. If your life can get better and if that's what you want, pursue your dream. You snooze, you lose. Take care."

"Thank you, Zica. You, too. Please, check on my mom whenever you can. Keep an eye at them for me. Call me if anything comes up."

They hugged and Zica was about to cry.

"Oh, no. Not you! Don't do that or I won't be able to make it."
"Let me cry! And you will get in that bus, or I'll slap you in the face!"
"You were so strong in my house!"
"Of course. When I came into your house, it looked like a funeral, everybody was crying. For God's sake! I had to try to lighten the mood".
"Let's keep the ball rolling. Chin up! Always!"
"I love you, my friend."
"I love you too, Zica."

The rain was stronger now and Zica's image was distorted between the raindrops that flowed down the bus window. He used his hand to defog the glass, he could still see his friend waving as the bus drove away. Life as he knew it was staying behind too. Everything was changing. And as he tired his neck from looking back, he straightened up on the bench and smiled as he looked forward.

> "Good afternoon, I'm Antonio from 401." He said to the doorman. José opened the door.
> "Here are the keys. Manuel, your landlord, left them here for you. You can use the service elevator, the door opens to the back door of the apartment, the laundry, where your bedroom is. This way, you'll have your own access to the apartment."
> "All right. Thank you very much."

The room was really very small. There was a single bed, right next to a two-door wardrobe and a small three-drawer dresser. No. There was no television as Antonio would have wanted, but it was clean and bright. There was no window, but daylight entered through the windows on the top of the wooden bedroom door. There was a bathroom only for him next door to the bedroom. The third door was the kitchen, which he could use and even store something on a designated refrigerator shelf that had been reserved for him. The building was well organized. There was a playground area with a swing and a slide. There were some iron benches on the garden, and that was all. He unpacked and carefully organized his wardrobe. He stored his books in the dresser. As his mother had predicted, the rain was pouring by then, and he could not go outside and explore the surroundings. Maybe on Sunday. He was all set. He closed the bedroom door, took a piece of the cake his grandmother made him, lit the little lamp, and lied on the bed with a book.

His new life had begun, but Antonio still did not know if it would be exactly as he expected. It was too early to tell. Everything was new, very different. But he had his own room in a beautiful neighborhood and there was even a garden in the building. He missed Piquito. He had to stay because the apartment owner did not like animals. That was one of the hardest things for Antonio. As much as Piquito did not speak, Antonio knew that they shared a connection that went beyond words. He missed his feathered friend, even though he did not speak. His presence brought him comfort. Was life always like that? Made of choices and more choices, decisions, losing, wining.... He felt like he was winning, but he also felt like he was losing.

"At the end of the day, everything is a lesson we learn. Be brave. Everything you need is inside you."

Chapter 10

From the Ecstasy to
the Theater Line

Sunday morning blossomed as if all the rain of the day before had just been a wet and distant dream. The sun shone, the sky was clear and blue. Felipe got up carefully not to wake his wife up. He peaked through the curtains and took a quick look at the beach. Then he went to his daughter's room, who was also asleep, like her mother. He went to the kitchen to prepare some coffee. A lonely Sunday morning ritual he always did when he was home. His unholy mass: no brushed teeth, no washed face, no speaking. Just the gestures. The silence.

From the balcony of his apartment, he could see the emerald green of the ocean, sprinkled with sun beams. Perfect day, perfect family. He could already predict the day: a walk by the beach on Ipanema, then the beach, lunch at the club, a chat with his friends in the afternoon, theater at night and, maybe they could squeeze in that "Sunday quickie". It did not seem like a bad plan. He laughed without smiling, just a slight stretch of the mouth. While steam spirals blended into the air, they lost their shape leaving the strong, intoxicating, irresistible smell of freshly prepared coffee in the air. Coffee beans freshly grounded by the machine he got from an Italian customer – another great connoisseur of the beverage – when he last went to Italy, during the European spring, his favorite season.

He pulled the chair in front of him and sat down. He raised his eyes out to the ocean, in that fraction of a second where everything goes through your head, but does not settle in. He looked again at the steamy cup. And following the rites he invented himself, he took a deep breath, pulling the air and aroma of coffee inside. It was the first step.

When he exhaled, he felt the first sign of relaxation. He took the cup, but it took him longer before he took it directly to his mouth. Not yet.

Like the foreplay before good sex, he circulated the nose across the surface, breathing shortly, almost a caress... he felt his body respond immediately, the gustatory pupils begged to be satisfied. Wet. The mouth waiting... He prolonged that for as long as he could. And passing his tongue through dry lips, he drank his first sip. Ecstasy.

"Oh, there you are with your little rituals. I don't know what you see in coffee, so early in the morning, without brushing your teeth. You don't even wash your face! So awful!" Gisella had just woken up and was desperately looking for something in the kitchen and was making a hell of a noise. Shrugging, he thought: "you can't have it at all".

\#\#\#\#\#\#

"Did you hear the mayor's last notice? He wants to raise property tax for the entire municipality."
"It seems that the city hall is down on money, as always, and the citizen pays the price, as always." One of them complained.
"Yeah! The middle class always pays the price" completed another one.
"Here comes the hottie with the snake tattoo," whispered a third one. They all turned to watch as the woman paraded.
"She's married. Did you see the wedding ring?"
"We're just looking. There's no harm."

They all agreed and after she and her snake tattoo gracefully turned to sit on the pool lounger, everyone sighed and turned their attention back to the table.

"Will you travel tomorrow? Where are you going to this time, Felipe? Where are you going to ask for money now?" Gustavo laughed. He loved to tease his friend after some drinks.
"I'm going to Buenos Aires tomorrow. I'll be back on Friday. If we win the bid and close the contract, we'll go to London at the end of the month. Two weeks.
"The luxury sales rep life!" His friend laughed and poked him.

"What matters to me is the commission!" He raised his eyebrows looking up while he laughed too. Felipe agreed. The fancy trips, five-star hotels, Michelin star restaurants where contracts were signed with the touch of the most exotic wines depending on the figures at stake. Italian ties, Armani suits, Ermenegildo Zegna perfumes. Everything was so seductive and exciting, but at the end of the day, he was a luxury sales rep indeed. With goals to meet, a boss on his neck and threats common to all sales professionals. From the boy selling candies at the traffic light to the CEO who wants to open the company's capital on the stock market. Everything was sales. Places, times and characters changed, but in the end it was all the same and if business did not go well, there would never be a shortage of sales reps' heads served in memos and recommendations for changes to soften the insatiable appetite for perpetual profits. It was part of the deal. The point was, he was a good sales rep. At home too, even though there were downsides to the married life, there was nothing out of the ordinary, except that there was something missing and he could not tell what. That feeling always came in at times when he had a break in his schedule, which basically meant the time he spent on flights, when he refused to open the laptop to look at the proposals for the last time. It started as a slightly uncomfortable feeling, easily cast away by some other practical problem. However, in the past years, it had become more resistant and showed up inconveniently without notice, robbing him of the continuity of conversations, like now.

"The stock's prices are good to enter the market with long-term plans."

He came from a traditional family. He was a well-educated man. His father had always been a demanding and conservative man with very strict principles that he inherited from his own father. Being a homeowner, having a united family, stability, keeping and increasing the family property were part of the Castro family commandments. Since he was a little boy, he had been educated to work in the family business and, in the future, take the place of his father. As an only son, an inherited responsibility, accompanied by laurels and whips rested on his shoulders. The laurels were the comfortable life he had. In fact, few people can say what wealth really is or is not. He had learned this lesson from his father.

"We are a financially stable family. A lot of people would even say we're rich. But notice that wealth is a gradient. You can be richer than one person and poorer than another. Anyway, after you have a certain amount of money, more than enough for your expenses, money is no longer a battle of life and death, you realize that true wealth is within you and that material wealth, at some point, loses its meaning. It doesn't bring happiness. It brings pleasures. It potentiates virtues and vices. Besides, the inner wealth I refer to is knowledge, emotional control, and the ability to think by yourself and solve problems.

One of the most famous sayings of the family doctrine, used by the old Agenor Castro, especially during lunches and festive gatherings was "We are rich because we solve more problems than we cause".

And that was bothering Felipe. He was afraid that weird feeling would cause him more trouble than he could solve.

"The problem is knowing the best time to enter the game." Completed Gustavo, his voice was distant.

Felipe didn't know when it had begun. He just liked being more involved with the simple things in life like the garden in his grandfather's cottage than necessarily with the commercial proposals he made. He liked plants, flowers, especially orchids and horses.

He spent much of his adolescent weekends away from car horns, crowds of people on sidewalks, the dark smoke of cars, and those common problems of large cities. Maybe that was the problem. He felt like his pace would slow down as he approached the dirt road and the veil of dust that led him to the small property the family owned in the mountain region of the state. It was a double effort: slowing down as he arrived at the house and speeding up on Monday morning to help the car odometer, and face another week of tests, work and traffic.

"You know that today is the quarterfinals of the Brasileirão Championship, right?" The subject on the table had already changed, but in his mind, the question was another.

The matter was that now, husband and father, he felt more and more compelled to stretch the weekend for at least another day of peace. Alone. No wife, no daughter, nothing. And he knew that little detail would be a problem. Not that he did not love them. Gisella was his first college girlfriend. She was beautiful, funny and had a yellow orchid smile that he picked up in that early spring of 1997. She cursed in French, a language she loved, but never had the discipline to learn well. She was a practical woman, she was dramatic and prone to confusion, with family and friends. He thought this was a natural spice to make social coexistence less monotonous. They fell in love. The families got along.

It seemed like the right thing to do. And there it was. After two years married, Julia was born with her 2.8 kilograms distributed throughout her chubby legs and arms. She was red-haired and had a w chin, just like him. The initially greyish eyes turned to sea green with a penetrating and curious look after two years of life, something she got from her mother. At that very moment he held the little package the doctor gave him, he felt all the fascination and miracle of life that his daughter represented. She was there, so small, so helpless. He felt an immense joy, and a great responsibility for that little person in his arms. His beloved Julia. He could not even imagine life without them.

"The dollar reached R$ 2.50! Do you think it will go higher or is that the highest it can go?"

Shame on him. He knew he should be ashamed of himself. A family like his, a life like his, their finances going so well. How dare he complain about life? He had everything anyone would dream of, but... something was not right... and he did not quite know what, but it was there. It was like one of those abstract paintings: after you see a shape, you can hardly see anything else. That was how he felt, even though he did not know why.

"Guys, I'm leaving." He finally said.
"It's early! Do you have any appointments?"
"I think we're going to the theater later. I

promised Gisella, and I have to take care of some things."

"All right. Claudio's birthday is coming and he's going to invite some friends for *drinks* at about eleven at the Marina da Gloria, but he will confirm two days before, because of the weather and tide conditions.

"When is it going to be?"

"Near the end of the month. Save the date."

"Ok. Good Sunday to you."

Later that night, the abstract figure of Felipe's imaginary painting would appear again, and he could finally give it a name.

Chapter 11

The word

On the other side of the city, Antonio also saw a painting in his mind. It was not abstract, it had well outlined contours. In a suit and tie, he entered the big multinational office building for the first time.

Two weeks had passed since he started preparing for the job interview in the company's headquarters. The imposing Argentina Building was in Botafogo, overlooking the small bay of the Botafogo Beach, at the foot of the Sugarloaf Mountain.

Many years had passed since he started working with Paulo at the city center. He chose a light shirt in his wardrobe. He had always liked walking when he was nervous. He had learned that a good walk was great for relaxing the mind, finding answers, and calming anxiety. Also, walking was free, which made it even more attractive. As the issue was very important, he thought that the walk deserved a better scenario than the silent streets of the Fatima district. And there was his connection to water; he could not explain it. He needed to see it, even in the distance, he needed the smell of the ocean air filling up his lungs.

Navy blue cargo shorts, a cap and sunglasses. It was a beautiful day for a walk in Copacabana.

He was afraid, there was no denying it. But he had come that far; It was not time to back off. Deep down he was more afraid to get the job than any other scenario. If he failed the interview, nothing would change, and things would continue as they were. He would not have to leave the old lawyer's office, where he started as an office-boy 10 years before, living in that bedroom in Méier. That was the first big turning point in his life, when he finally managed to get out of the favela. It is funny how sometimes it feels like dreams change, but that is not quite what happens. Dreams never change if they are true. They are the same, only that there are different levels. After he managed to get out of the favela, he wanted to move to a better neighborhood, maybe a small studio apartment, then a small apartment with one bedroom. Who knows, maybe one day he would even be able to own a place. Dreams change shape, but never their essence. The only thing that did not change was that for some dreams to come true he needed money. That new job opportunity could be the key to that dream. He would work in the international contracts sector and the position would pay twice what Paulo paid him as a junior lawyer. He did not want to look ungrateful. After all, with Paulo's advice and support guiding Antonio he had been accepted into law school. Even though Paulo did not pay for his tuition, he gave Antonio much more: all the books, tips, extra help with the studies and mentoring.

However, he felt he could not let that opportunity

pass. He always thought life was unfair. He always had to choose between one thing or another. That had happened when he left home 15 years before: leaving the love and warmth of his mother's home and his grandmother's affection for his dream of changing his life and living in a beautiful place. He never regretted anything, but it broke his heart when a few years later his mother called to say his grandmother had suffered a massive heart attack while praying. It was all too fast, she said. They had just finished reading some passages of the Bible and they were saying their final prayers. Suddenly, she heard her mother let out a small moan as her hand squeezed hers. The grip gradually loosened, until she felt Maria's hand go cold. She opened her eyes, but she could no longer see her mother alive. Perhaps an almost imperceptible smile but she could not say for sure. The problem with death is that whether it comes with a warning or not, we are never prepared for it. Losing his second mother hurt a lot, but more than that, it hurt him not having been there to say goodbye. As she died praying, he liked thinking that maybe the conversation with God was so good that He decided to call her so they could continue the conversation in person. Every choice involves a loss. That was a lesson he learned early.

So far away, he barely noticed when the bus crossed the tunnel that separated Botafogo and Copacabana. He got off the bus right after the tunnel and headed towards the boardwalk. For the those born in the city, few things are more beautiful than a sunny Sunday in Rio de Janeiro with its deep and incredibly blue sky touching the green waters and strong waves of the Atlantic as it washes the shore. People walking, exercising, or drinking coconut water at the kiosks was a perfect combination of the city's natural beauties with the lifestyle that only coastal city dwellers can understand. The place was still the same. He was the one who had changed. There was not much left of that boy who could barely say a few memorized English sentences to sell theater tickets. He had concluded his English course and was now studying Spanish. He had always liked languages. He was good at them.

How could he know that his childhood dream would change his life so much? He began to understand, or at least he thought so, that life really begins to happen when we take the first step and continue walking towards our dream. He himself could not believe that an ignorant slum dweller who just wanted to live in a beautiful place was about to graduate from college against all odds. It was not something you saw every day, even though he was there. And he knew the story was real. Those college years were combined with temporary jobs as a hotel receptionist because of his good English. There was only enough money to pay for his expenses, there was never any money left, a reality for most college students.

Perhaps working at the hotel helped him to

develop a taste for traveling and adventure. It was nice to see all those different people all the time. He had fun wondering where they came from as they filled out the check-in card. What would it be like to fly? At that time everything seemed so far from his reality. With time and experience, he saw that the only way to make his dream come true would be to have a very good job and a little bit of luck.

As he walked by the Copacabana Fort, he admired the unique view of the entire of Copacabana Beach, its golden sands dotted by the colorful tents and beach umbrellas.

He recalled Paulo's words: *"Pay attention, boy. A lot of people are waiting for good luck to magically take them by their hands. That looks good in movies and soap operas, but the probability of that happening is virtually zero and you need to be smarter than that. In real life, good luck is like that beautiful capricious girl who needs to be courted and seduced to be with you. By doing your part, and technically preparing, acquiring knowledge and being bold, you become a more interesting and attractive suitor. Thus, you're the one who reaches out to her"*.

And it was true. He used his breaks during his hotel shifts to learn not only good manners at the table, but also how to behave in social classes different from his, their tastes and manners. He would observe the guests and colleagues and could count with *maître* Luizão, who generously corrected him and suggested books. Who knew, maybe one day he would be invited to put it all into practice. Anyway, he would do his part, as his lawyer friend said. He would do his part and reach out for good luck.

All those years of patience and dedication seemed to begin to bear fruit. The single room in Méier had evolved into a small studio apartment in the Fatima District. He did not mind working extra jobs on the weekends so he could pay the rent. Also, he saved on transportation from work to college since both were at a walking distance.

If he were too hungry and had a little money left, he would go to the popular restaurant behind the clock in the Central do Brasil Station, where the food was very good. The only challenge was the clientele, since the restaurant was a government initiative to help the homeless and the less assisted with a balanced and dignified meal at the symbolic cost of R$1. When he got hungry and had no money, a large glass of water would have to do it.

He was very fond of his neighborhood. There were large almond trees lining the streets and their leaves provided precious shadows on hot days. One of his favorite Saturday morning activities was going to the local street market. There was all the talking, and the smell of fried pastel[1], new lemon and fresh cilantro were his favorites. A perfect street market must have pastel and, of course, sugar cane juice. He had been living there for two years and he could not have chosen a better place among the neighborhoods he could afford. Was it tiny? Twelve meters square. It was tiny indeed. There was only one window overlooking the street and the side of a large synagogue and its geometrical and colorful rose window. There was a bathroom and space for a two-burner stove. He had to buy a fridge and a sofa bed. Not bad for someone who left home just with a backpack. The prices we pay... If he had to work on weekends so he could live there, so be it. Nothing in his life was easy and it would be no different now.

Under the shadow of one of the almond trees in the Fort, he picked the sandwich he had packed before leaving home. And as the waves monotonously reached the sand, he wondered what would happen next. Well, if he did well in that interview, his life would change a lot. Was he ready for another change? What if he was not? What if he made it and then did not pass the trial period? What if he passed the trial period and then did something wrong and got fired? What if they did not like him?

Things were safer and quieter with Paulo. He knew how to do things and how to behave. He knew the

---

[1] A typical fast-food Brazilian food consisting of half-circle or rectangle-shaped thin crust pies with assorted fillings, fried in vegetable oil.

way Paulo liked the job done. It was all very predictable and, who knows, maybe he would reach a senior lawyer position there. That was quite possible. He would make a career there until he retired. It did not seem like a bad plan. And it really was not.

He could not explain that feeling. Something inside him pulled him somewhere he did not know. He was indeed grateful for everything he had achieved. He was proud of his history and everything he had been through. The bad times, difficulties, and adventures too. Like the first time he secretly tried some of Paulo's whiskey. He wanted to imitate the old lawyer, reciting poems, and giving lessons on the paintings hanging on the walls. Everything was going great until he took his first sip. Bitter and strong, the whiskey came down burning. He started sweating and, in fear of getting caught, left the room to drink water, but he was dizzy. Lucky for him, a maid saw the situation, and after a good laugh, she helped him cover up his petty crime, of course he had to promise her it was the first and last time he would do that. That would not be hard after that that screw-up.

Good memories... but he did not feel like that life was meant for him. And he felt lost. Was he being ungrateful? Should he be thankful for the luck he had to get there? Luck so many others did not have. . . What is the limit of a dream? When is it enough? Would he be pushing his luck too hard, as in the myth of Icarus, who in an attempt to reach the skies, flew so high that the sun heat melted the wax wings he had built? Was he the favela Icarus who wanted to touch the sun of a better life and was about to plummet?

He was afraid. And he was also hopeful, in the same proportion. From another perspective, he had come out of nowhere, he had been through a lot, more times than he could remember, and he was still there. It was better to try and fail than regret not trying.

He took the last bite of the sandwich, noting the many boats and their sails that seemed to be in some sort of competition on their route far away from the designated swimmers' area.

He remembered reading somewhere that each one of us has come into the world to discover our own word. The word that would give meaning to our entire existence. And when you discovered it and said it, you would die, just like the legend of the Greek runner who died of exhaustion after running 42 kilometers to announce the victory of Athens, after uttering the word: "Victory."

A plane was approaching the Santos Dumont Airport. As he saw it, Antonio discovered what his word was. Now he needed the courage to say it and die.

Chapter 12

The Picture

"Come on, babe. If there's traffic, we'll arrive at the last minute and I'll still have to park the car."
"Almost! Just a minute I'm finishing my makeup."
"Okay, the sitter is already with Julia."

He did not know what play they were going to watch. He left it to Gisella, who had more time and enjoyed it more. He liked the theater, but it was not his passion. He preferred the races and a good book with a cup of coffee. These were his so called "little pleasures". On the way to the Lagoa, he saw a thin and shirtless boy who juggled and balanced lemons at the traffic light. He counted seven lemons. Up and down, spinning in the air like the plastic balls from those ball pools at kids' parties. Are we all like that boy? Balancing the lemons life gives us without dropping them in exchange for a few bucks? He had his contracts to close. He felt like that boy, but he never thought of that. Sometimes people are invisible, on the margins... On the edge... Put aside... We go past them, and we do not see them. Like they had never been there, as if they were undead in a zombie society. Who knew, maybe was also a zombie, living his perfect life, going from one place to another, without a destination? Wandering. A zombie. Or the contrary, perhaps he knew exactly where he would end up. He would end up running his family's business, as one of the many sequences of that movie, as the portraits of his great-great-grandfathers in the living room of his father's house, as a graphic and natural script to be followed effortlessly.

"Do you have R$10?"
"I do. Why?"
"Give it to me. Quick."
"Here, I only have a 20."
"That will do."

He opened the car window, he waved for the boy, who came in a hurry.

"There you go. You have a talent."
"Thank you, boss. You know, we do what we have to do."
"That's right!" He answered laughing.
"You shouldn't encourage that. You know that, right?" Gisella reprehended Felipe, as soon as the boy walked away. "It's too risky to open the car windows at a traffic light. It's safer for you to donate to some serious entity that takes care of it."
"But I wanted to talk to him. Thank him."
"Thank him for what, Felipe, have you gone crazy?"
"We're all jugglers. We're all juggling on the avenues of life, babe."

"Oh... Here you come with those ideas of yours. Come on, if we're late, it'll be your fault."

"Always, dear. That's called marriage!" He was in a good mood and was not going to start an argument for nothing. At that moment he preferred the peace of a smile while gently touching his wife's leg.

The atmosphere in the theater was very pleasant. The powerful air conditioning kept the temperature to what Felipe thought was about 22°C. The ideal temperature for the proper functioning of the human body, according to him, unlike the 42°C outside. Even if he did not like the play, being there was already a good thermal reward.

The play was a Brazilian adaptation of Oscar Wilde's *The Portrait of Dorian Gray*. He remembered the title of one of those movies available on airplanes, but the story had never drawn his attention. He knew it had something to do with the Greek myth of Narcissus and selling the soul to the devil in exchange for eternal beauty. Since he was not fond of fables and myths, he had never cared to learn about them. He liked practical things that could be used immediately and could not see a practical application for Greek myths or epic poems. He liked biographies of great personalities, if not based on, at least inspired by real facts. He considered himself a hopeful realist. He expected the best, but without closing his eyes to reality, whatever it was. And yes, that was the story he thought it would be. Those were going to be two very long hours!

In the Brazilian version, Dorian was played by a beautiful young man in his late twenties, he had fair eyes, shoulder length hair and was very charming. The theater was full, and the first bell had already rung. They sat in their comfortable crimson velvet armchairs. The pressure of a thumb could leave a gentle mark the surface of that velvet due to its softness.

Second bell.

The curtains open. A young man walks around the stage like he is walking in a park, or would it be a forest? The scenery was dark, distorted shapes resembled the shadows of trees and leaves projected on the background, or could it be a projection of his inner mental state? If so, the character reflected peace and beauty. It was a harmonious set.

Why did he agree to go to the theater without even checking on the play before? He could have given an excuse or suggested something else. He would be trapped there for at least two hours, there was no way he could escape it now. What could he do? He peered at Gisella who was completely attentive to the spectacle. Yes, he was alone in that one. Turning his eyes, he sighed and looked at the stage to see what was happening. The light had changed and now the actor was saying: "... that everything is so common..."

He did not hear the rest of it, he began thinking about the contract to be signed the next day in Buenos Aires. The numbers were good and if everything worked out fine, by the end of the month, he would be in London for formalizations. Maybe he could stretch that trip to another day or two and enjoy the capital. Hopefully, he could even try to watch a race. The horses! Yes, he would have the opportunity to see how the English took care of the animals. That would be interesting. Too bad he could not devote more of his time to that. Who knew, maybe one day...

"Are you enjoying it?"

He did not realize, lost in his thoughts, that the first act was over and the lights were on, thus allowing viewers to get up if they wanted to go to the restrooms or buy something in the theater café.

"Yes. Very interesting." He lied more out of inertia than will, surprised by the interruption of his flow of thoughts.
"I'll go to the restroom. Do you want anything from the café?"
"I'll go. I need to stretch my legs too. Thank you."
"*Whiskey on the rocks*, please."

"How many rocks?"

"Three. The whiskey over the ice. Thank you."

The watery and bitter taste of the drink felt good for him. Gradually he felt relaxed while his cheeks became slightly warm and sensitive.

Someday...

Would he really have the time to do something he really liked? He had the financial stability to do most of the things he wanted to do. The problem was that he could not find anything that got his attention. One contract after another, one day after another, meetings, projects. It was all very normal and logical. But most of the time he was not really there. Just like now. He was there and he was not. As in funeral masses, his soul wandered. Everything made a lot of sense to everyone but him. A part of him liked the idea of stability and continuation that a picture of him on his father's living room wall would bring. The other half suffocated when he thought of himself trapped and inexpressive on that wall, another piece in a collection of memories, so predetermined that they all looked the same. He was constantly torn between conforming or trying something different. And there were choices to be made. But he was too lazy to choose. Or a coward. On the other hand, maybe it was just a midlife crisis. Forty years go by fast and psychologists say that, at this stage, many things go through our minds and that it was all very natural. He hoped so, this way nothing would have to be different from what had been planned for his life.

"Sir, the second act will begin." The waiter informed him.

"Oh, yes. Thank you. I'll go back to my seat."

####

"How sad it is! I shall grow old, and horrible, and dreadful!" Exclaimed the actor who played Dorian. Eyes fixed on the picture that depicted the character in all his physical glory. "For that – for that – I would give everything! Yes, there is nothing in the whole world I would not give! I would give my soul for that!"

Those last words caught Felipe's attention, he also had eyes fixed on the painting, but what he saw, away from the painting they had placed on the set was his own portrait. Old and dusty until it was not even a memory anymore. "What if things could be different?" He repeated that in his mind weighing the words. However, for that to happen, he would need a passion, a dream, a project. Something that would push him to beyond himself, forward. The courage to make the necessary choices needed to be awakened. But first, he had to know what he really wanted. And that was holding him back and bothering him lately. His great-grandfather seemed to know what he wanted, and his will was so strong that it prevailed for generations driving everyone's lives, like his father's. He seemed satisfied with the life he led, of course. Felipe, on the contrary, felt out of place. It was like he lacked purpose. But that might just be another fad: the "marketing of purpose"? Whatever it was, the question bothered him for real. He felt like he was withering away, like the picture. Even if outside, everyone saw him in his glory, only he knew his reverse. The abstract image was taking his shape. He just was not sure which side he was looking at.

Later, on his way home, he teased his wife: "Honey, can I ask you a question?"

"Sure, what is it?"
"What's your biggest dream?"
"Sorry?"
"What's the biggest dream of your life?"
"What kind of question is that Felipe?"
"Just answer. What's the big deal?"

She looked up as if she was trying to help her memory. Gisella took a deep breath and answered slowly, but in a steady voice: "I wanted to be a mother, have my family and be happy."

"Yes, but that's the basics. I mean, like, what else? A personal project, something meaningful, you know?"

"And what can be more meaningful than my family and my happiness?"

Felipe silently absorbed her words. He did not expect that answer. He was hoping she would say something else. Something like a secret wish, a major project. That simple answer, especially speaking of the family, baffled him. Was she right after all and he was complicating things? What about the happiness part? If it were true, something was wrong, because after all, he did not feel completely happy. He found this notion of happiness his wife mentioned to be naïve. As a single planet that needed to provide finite resources for the infinite desires of more than eight billion human beings. He was happy enough, and maybe that was it. He was not sure. In fact, the more he thought about it, the more doubts he had. However, the idea of dreams being pursued seemed more attractive and doable than fully enjoying them. Who knew that happiness would be diluted in the achievements and failures we experience as we pursue a dream?

"What about you?" His wife wanted to know.
"The same." And that was half-true. Deep down, he was not sure if the dreams referred to the full happiness of the family or something else that he also did not know yet or did not have the guts to find out.
"You took too long to answer. Is everything all

right, love?" She asked as she raised her left eyebrow, one of her trademarks.

"Yes. Just thinking."

"Did you see how you give nothing to tales and myths, but sometimes they bring many internal truths if you pay attention?"

"Yes, maybe. But don't you come on now with the Wizard of Oz! Please!" He changed the subject.

"You know nothing! The dialogues of this work contain so much wisdom between the lines! Most people think it's just a book when it's more like three! People just read the first layer."

"Okay, okay... Maybe one day. . ."

Chapter 13

Icarus

It was the first time he had ever set foot in an airport. He could not believe it! He felt like he was in a movie. Was this really happening? Was it real? It felt like the 14-year-old Antonio was jumping up and down inside his chest, and a wide open boy smile denounced him as he passed through shops, *stands*, suitcases, carts, flight announcements, wheels that passed over people's feet. People were well dressed, tidy, choreographed. So was he.

How could he know that the interview a week before was only the first of two interviews and the last one would be at the São Paulo branch, which was exactly where he was going. If he passed that interview, he would be hired! Everything was finally working out for him! He reached out to luck and it seemed to be coming towards him. He could feel it! He would get it!

He felt like he was floating on his way to the airplane. It seemed like a dream, but this one was very real. As he buckled his seat belt, he looked through the window. He took his phone and called his mother right away. It was so much happiness and he needed to share it with her. Even though they did not live together, they kept in touch. Fortunately, the man his mother had started flirting with a little before his grandmother's death became a husband, and soon there would be another member to the family. A few months earlier, Ana had been born. The name was chosen by him as requested by his mother. Sometimes he wondered if he would have had the strength to leave the house if his sister had come before he did. He always wanted someone to play with when he was little. He was lonely. He had just realized that now.

"Your blessing, mother!"

"God bless you, son! How are you?"

"Great!" He felt he was about to cry. "Guess where I am right now?"

"Where?"

"I'm going to São Paulo, by plane, for a job interview!"

There was a silence on the other side of the line for a second.

"Mom! Can you hear me? Mom?"

"Plane? Why not the bus? Where did you get the money? Are you okay? Oh, my God. You're crazy, Antonio!"

"Mom, I made it! I'm flying! From now on, every time you look at the sky, you'll know that one day I've been up there, above the clouds!" The sunglasses hid the tears, but the buttons of the jacket going up and down denounced the sobs he was trying to contain. The growing sound of the engines hid his crying.

"Sir, you need to turn off your phone."

"Sure. I'm sorry."

"Mom, I have to go now."

"I am very proud of you, son. If it's meant to be, it'll be. God bless you!"

"Kisses. Bye!"

####

"Alguma coisa acontece no meu coração..." the song Caetano Veloso wrote to show his affection for the capital of São Paulo was a sweet warning that they were about to land in the Congonhas Airport. The airline's idea of playing this song onboard a few minutes before landing in São Paulo was a nice touch.

We keep many scenes in our minds, and this was one Antonio kept. He was looking through the window when the plane finished its curve and he could see São Paulo grow in all its urban grandiosity, a jungle of buildings and humans. Its infinite skyscrapers reflected the sunlight as if they were giant lighthouses. The strong sun beams hit windows and metal structures that stretched as far as his eyes could see. He had never seen anything like it. São Paulo made him feel small. He was afraid.

During the taxi ride to the office he began to feel

better. All those buildings... There was a place waiting for him. And he was going to get it!

The interview was over. Now he needed to wait for them to call. There were other candidates for the job, and they said they would call in an hour. He was about to board the plane when the phone rang.

"Hello. Is that Antonio?"
"Speaking."
"Good afternoon. I'm calling regarding the open position with our company. We would very much like to thank you for your time, but we decided to go with another candidate that we think is more suitable for this position. Thanks."
"You are welcome." The adrenaline rush that went through Antonio's spine when he answered the phone soon became a torpor when the secretary started uttering the word "but"... Nothing good comes after "but" in a situation like that. He felt like he was going to break down.

The higher the plane got, the more he shrunk into his seat. Looking down, he was wondering if he would ever fly again. After all that, his dream was over. How come? He looked at the clouds and the earth below, and Antonio could not believe it. He felt so sure after those weeks of preparation, study, energy, positive thinking. He had done everything right and, in the end, he failed. He felt lost, helpless, a victim of life's injustices. Everything was lost now. He would not go anywhere, and he would have to retire as a lawyer in the same firm. How did those great plans leave such a bitter taste in his mouth? Or was it the salt of the tears coming down?

Chapter 14

New Year's Eve

"Nothing like one day after another and a night in the middle to get in the way."

That had always been his mother's favorite saying. Simple but profound. A saying that reminded him of the resilience and great strength we find when we decide to pursue something, even though we have a chance to go back. However, in the middle, there was the "night to get in the way". And some nights lasted more than twelve hours. The big problem is facing the night. Going through it. Getting over it. It is not something that can be taught or learned. And Antonio walked through it the way he knew, by working, studying, waiting, despairing, dreaming. When would another chance come?

How many years had passed since that flight to São Paulo, in which he felt at the top of the world? Had sadistic luck pretended to have finally opened a door for him, giving him a glimpse of how his life could be and all it could offer, just to then slam that door in his face? Five years already? That still felt like yesterday. But his life had changed so much since then. Nothing could have impacted and changed him as much as Paulo's death three years before. A deadly and silent tracheal cancer developed for more than two years in the body of the old lawyer. First damaging his speech, then weakening his body, then the little hair he still had losing the battle against the chemotherapy. Only his spirit seemed to resist, and he saw it the last time they met. It was a sad visit, but he taught him one of the greatest lessons he could learn, and that lesson will be kept in a special place in his heart forever.

Intubated, Paulo could no longer speak. Therefore, with difficulty, he used a small white clipboard on which he wrote short sentences; the act of taking the marker and drawing the letters was painful and there was the risk of losing the access to his already weakened veins, the price he paid for the strong medications. But before they said goodbye, he approached the lawyer to shake his hand, instead, Paulo indicated that he wanted the clipboard. His handwriting was shaky, but strongly traced and it revealed the indelible and meaningful message:

"Live until you die."

At that moment, Antonio understood that it was necessary to live until he died. And that meant acting, trying, failing and trying in different ways until he got it. That man who he met so many years before and who changed not only the way he saw life, but also his own life was lying there, so close to death. He who mentored him through life, still had one last lesson for Antonio. Live until you die! Do not give in. Resist. Continue. And the strength of Paulo's spirit was there saying that he would continue living until the last moment.

People also become immortal when they give us their wisdom and are part of our life and worldview. They live inside us. Paulo's words would live in Antonio.

The distant fireworks startled him. It was New Year's Eve. Life goes by so fast.

####

Ten days turn into ten months. Ten months turn into ten years. Squeezed in the sands of the Copacabana Beach, thousands of people predominantly dressed in white, struggling for a place to watch the firework display. The distraction brought Antonio's eyes to the noisy crowd, who sang, argued, danced, and clapped their hands. On the opposite side of the beach, he saw the balconies of the buildings of Atlantica Avenue and their bright and festive penthouses. Everybody was waiting. Waiting.

He had waited for so long. All those years. How many more? Things changed after Paulo died. The old man was the heart of the firm and when it stopped beating, it would only be a matter of time before the cyanosis of his absence gave way to the organs, and multiple failures. His extra weekend jobs saved him, but they were not enough to pay the rent. Two months later the office closed and before he could not pay the rent, he had to make a decision:

"Mom, I need to ask you something."

"Sure. What's it?"

"The firm closed, and I haven't found another job yet. The money I make in the hotel is not enough for the rent and bills."

"Stay here. At least until you get back on your feet. This house has always been and will always be yours. I know it's in the favela, but it's a roof over your head, son. Come home."

"Thank you, mom." He hung up before she noticed he was about to cry. He did not want his mother to know how sad and disappointed he was. But life was hard for everyone. The problem was that he had had a glimpse of how life could be different and beautiful, and that image would not leave him. He had lost his soul, the first time he found himself on a plane glancing at the earth from above. He had crossed a barrier that seemed impossible. He had managed to fly and be interviewed by a reputable law firm. He knew it was possible. He now wanted to turn that possibility into a probability.

Years went by and the odds did not change much.

"Thief! Thief!" Someone shouted in the distance.

And that was the image to which he clung when he got off the bus and began walking back to his mother's house in the favela. Ten years had gone by since that day he said goodbye to Zica at that same bus stop. He never thought he would go back to that place for more than a visit. And that walk to the door of the house was one of the heaviest ones of his life. He left that place full of hope and dreams all those years before and now he was coming back felling like a foolish and ridiculous loser. Antonio and his books, and his crazy wishes for a better life were back in the favela. Everything had gone down the drain. Just like the smell of fresh cilantro in the Saturday street market giving way to the foul and forgotten smell of the open-air sewage dreadfully welcoming him back. Life was much more real than TV commercials picture it. Not all endings are happy ones.

And who knew, after all those years, Zica was right: no studies, no diplomas, nor great ambitions, being happy was a fad, pursuing happiness elsewhere other than inside us was a mistake since there were too many people seeking for it, and she was sure that there should not be happiness for everyone, and most people were poor.

Antonio, between reality and the dream, chose the dream, not because he was sure, he was too sad to be sure. He chose the dream because it was stronger than him. The idea that he could be and have more tormented him.

A wise proverb says that anything that is really

worth it takes time. And as time passed and he did not get a job in law, Antonio used his time to learn another profession. He liked computers and was a fast learner. He was in the fourth year of law school when his life turned upside down. Paulo died and the firm was closed. He had to drop out of college.

Computer science was a promising career, and everyone said it was the future. The fact was that there was a technical course that cost less than going to law school and he could get a paid internship while studying. He did not think twice, once he did not have to pay rent, he could do it. Thus, he combined his knowledge of law and oratory to bits and bytes and became a well-articulated business analyst. He waited sometime after he consolidated his career to make sure that no serious setback in life would make him return to his mother's shelter and he rented a small studio apartment in Copacabana. Later, he got a job as a technology consultant at a large Brazilian company, then took another opportunity to become national sales manager for an oil multinational until he finally became that regional manager for Latin America at another multinational company in the same segment.

He never thought he would make it that far. He just he kept doing the best he could, completely absorbed by the view that life could be more… that he could be more.

"Ten, nine..."

He picked up the sparkling wine and a glass in his bag. He nearly forgot it was almost midnight.

"Eight, seven..."

The noise of the firecrackers was almost deafening. All that excitement. People jumping in waves...

"Six, five..."

A naked woman eating grapes went into the sea. "Four, three..."

The lit cruise ships in the bay began flashing in the distance.

"Two, one..."

An explosion of light and sound, screams, applause made Rio's night brighter than the day in one of the most beautiful places in the world to be on New Year's Eve.

"Happy New Year!"

"For you too, dear." Felipe told his wife as he pulled her for a kiss.

"Daddy, look what I've done!" Sophia ran towards him with a scribbled leaf, where an animal, a house and three human figures held hands.

"What is it, love?"

"The horse, the horse's house."

"It's called a stud farm, daughter." He corrected her with affection.

"Stud farm," she repeated, "me, you and mom!"

"Very beautiful! What's that on the corner?"

"It's a star!"

"But only one?"

"It is grandpa in heaven." She replied with the softness and simplicity that only children have in such a situation.

"That's all right. Where's your aunt?"

"I don't know. I'll look for her."

"Very well. But first... Where's my kiss?"

Time never seemed to pass. He had lost his father five years before and it felt like it was yesterday! They say that grief softens over time, but for Felipe, time had not passed. He felt the presence of his father. Especially when he visited his mother. Perhaps because his painting, the one that had been ready before and was exposed at his funeral, rested on its assigned place, next to his ancestors. And so, his memory was always there. He could not forget the last conversation they had before the accident that took his father away. "You have an obligation to this family, Felipe. Your great-great-grandfather, before your great-grandfather, and your grandfather, and I have been faithful to this legacy, and you will not change the order established long before you were born, young man! This legacy is greater than you, me, or any of us." He knew the words they had exchanged by heart and they tortured him.

"But, dad, why does it have to be one thing or another? Why does one idea exclude the other? Can't we make a deal?"
"Son, you're not going to be a horse seller, stinking of manure and stable. That's not what I dreamed for you or for the family legacy."
"But, dad, it's not a question of money anymore. I found out I like the place and the horses, and I think the stud farm could unite these two passions and yield a good income as well. And that's what's happening."

At that point, the call was interrupted. Felipe's father, distracted by the conversation, had not noticed that he had changed lanes and was driving the wrong way on Niemeyer Avenue and hit a bus coming in the opposite direction, right after the curve before the overpass. The doctors said he died immediately.

He felt completely guilty for what happened and never told anyone what they were talking about. He said it was business, but he knew it was not exactly that. If only he had not started the stud farm project... Despite being a true case of success, it had caused a profound rupture in their relationship dynamics. At first, he did not want to know anything about the office, but after thinking, he decided he could do both. Even so, he felt his father's disappointment, sometimes concealed, and others, quite explicit. He felt the looks of disapproval for the prizes he won, and the disparaging comments sprinkled with strong bitterness.

After the funeral, he did not feel like running the business. The guilt he felt followed him everywhere. Deep down he wanted to go back in time, and he knew exactly where: that damn moment where he flipped through the pages of an obscure book he had found in a small bookstore a few years before. The book told the story of an executive who had dropped everything to pursue the dream of becoming a writer. What was the name…? Oh... Something like *Courage to Dream*, he guessed. The story had inspired him in such a way that he gathered his courage and decided to chase after his dream. At the time he knew he wanted to turn the place into a stud farm. He could not tell his father. That was the moment he wanted to go back to, he wished he had never gone into that bookstore. But time does not stop, it does not go back either.

The months went by and the depression settled in. The unwillingness, lack of spirit, desire. A natural sadness was gaining space, shape and like that picture, in that play he had seen years ago, his soul seemed deformed due to pain and guilt, far beyond what others could see. He knew that he needed to react, but he had no strength, no will. He felt like he had disappointed his father and, more than that, caused his death. He needed to get himself together, or all his family had fought for would have been for nothing. In other times, he could have taken the car and sought refuge in the peace of the stud farm. But he had sold it for peanuts, as they say. There was nothing left. Anyways, he thought the New Year could bring fresh air and watching the last fireworks and people moving through the sands of Leblon, he noticed a small group that had lit an area of the beach with white candles, while some devotees sent small boats with flowers into the sea, he felt like he was also a boat on the ocean. He wanted to be a boat and disappear in the ocean night following the silver path lit by the full moon.

The air that came out of his nostrils and mouth was heavy when he took the last sip of the sparkling wine. Next week, he would go to Paris for work and the aroma of the Parisian cafes of the Marais always had the power to bring his spirits up. He hoped so. After all: "It takes a lot of effort to feel depressed in Paris," one of his wife's favorite sayings. For her, no place was more charming than Paris.

Laissez les bon temps rouler.

Chapter 15

Choices and Farewells

"Whiskey, on the rocks, three rocks, please." Antonio asked to the flight attendant. One of the many advantages of the executive class was the board service that started on soil. He placed the glass on the tray, then got up to go to the restroom. The trip to England would take eleven hours and the many *drinks* of his farewell party the night before urged him to go. On his way to the restroom, he saw a woman that looked like Zica, but it was not her, of course. Where would she be? Zica was one of those unpredictable characters. Although she said she loved living where she lived, it was impossible to tell. But he heard from his mother that her hot dog business had flooded … into coconut water. Oh... in the end she found a partner who already had about ten coconut water sales points at the beach! It seemed that she had her sales points now too. Too bad she did not go to his farewell party. When would he see her now? If he would ever see her again.

More relieved, he took his seat and picked up his glass. This was a very special day, and it deserved a whiskey, as Paulo would have liked one. He was moving to England exactly ten years after Paulo died, a sad coincidence. He looked out the window. A thin drizzle and heavy clouds covered the Church of Penha so he could not see it as he took off. Neither could he see the Christ the Redeemer. He had been saying goodbye to the city for a couple of weeks, little by little, by glancing at those streets, or when watching the elderly on the streets of his neighborhood. He already missed everything, even though he was still there. Goodbyes...

Nothing was harder than leaving his mother and sister in the departure lounge. They had arrived early to check his luggage. It was not much. But it was more than the first time he left home. Instead of that backpack, he now had two bags of thirty-two kilograms each. They talked for two hours before boarding and everything seemed fine until it was time to go.

Before they could open their mouths to rehearse a word, they both fell into each other arms crying, convulsive, as if they had sharp knives in their chests. Maybe that is why they say the heart hurts. It must be the combination of the feelings and the flesh, with our body.

There was nothing to be said. What can you say to tears at times like those?

The first time and then the second time he left home were goodbyes. But now he was going to another country, not a half an hour away by bus. But they were there. The biggest of his choices. He was going to leave the country to go somewhere beautiful in England. It was the realization of a dream, of a project. How many times had he dreamed of that moment! He just had not thought of the final goodbye. He was not ready for that. Neither one of them. Every day, years, defeats, disappointments, failures, depression, were sacrificed. Luck, that capricious girl, had opened the door to an opportunity to live abroad. He had saved some money and he would take a chance again. He could not live with the feeling of not trying. He knew what his word was. He had to say it and die there to be reborn in a new world, a new phase. He regained his voice. He wavered. Between sobs he could say:

"You know I need to do this, don't you? What if..."
"I know, son!" His mother did not let him finish. She cried and hugged him as strong as she could. Deep down, it was like she was saying goodbye to herself. And she wanted to go too, while holding her son so tight as if she was trying stop herself.

"Passengers of the flight to London, please board at Gate 9."

He could not breath right. It was time.

"I have to go, mom."

"Go, son. God bless you! I'm proud of the man you've become."

He turned and stared at the gate. He was not able to look back. The toll of another goodbye was too heavy for him. And now his choice took him again to a new level into the unknown. He had no idea what to expect. But he had already made it that far. He had nothing to lose that he had not won and lost on his journey. He had learned that everything was going to pass.

And now a new chapter of his life began. The plane went higher and higher, until it broke through the cloud ceiling, and made them the new ground beneath a beautiful blue sky. Curiously, even when the clouds are heavy and dense and you can fly above them, you realize that the sky is always blue. It could be the title of his new book: "The Sky Is Always Blue." Oh, yes, the book. He needed to review the English version that the translator had sent. Who knew that one day he would have listened to his mother's idea of writing a book about his life? So many years had passed since he decided to leave the favela and everything seemed somewhat distant, almost like a dream, the kind you have when you sleep. Besides, he thought the story of a poor boy that changes his life was so cliché. People would prefer more miraculous stories about rich people, like those of football players, billionaire businesspeople and TV stars. He was nothing like that, neither in terms of fame – he was not understood by most people – nor in terms of money.

The day after he quit his job to move abroad, he dreamed of his dear friend Paulo and that poem of his, the one that went, "It is not for nothing…" He woke up startled, he could remember only one word or another. Something about "he wouldn't understand" or "planting seeds"... Nothing was really clear... remembering things can be funny, because we never remember exactly how they were... only parts, the most memorable... but even them, after years and years, seem more like something sketched by pencil... opaque and hazy images, as if they were a film of someone else's life... like the clouds he saw through the window... appearing and disappearing. Shapeless, dissipating in the deep blue of the unconsciousness.

And there he was. A suitcase and a dream of *some beautiful place to live in peace*, as in Roberto Carlos' song, *Além do Horizonte*.

It had been a busy day. In fact, the last few days had been busy. There were last minute problems to solve, packing. Not that any of it was new to his routine. He was used to traveling, VIP lounges and welcome drinks. It was just that this trip would be different. He needed to seal a very important deal. They all were. He knew the carrot and donkey game and he was sick of carrots. But he had to go on with his life; it would not stop because of his problems, even though he sometimes wanted it to, as we all do when we are hurting and sad. Even so, the ruthless life shrugged and continued to exist demanding the fulfillment of previously agreed commitments.

On his way to the airport, he took one last look at the busines proposal and the numbers to see that they were consistent and closed the laptop. He refused to work during the flight. He would enjoy the flight to London as he usually did, and that was just the first part of it. A connection to Paris awaited him. So, if the proposal needed to be adjusted, he would wait until he landed at London Heathrow Airport to do it.

Passing by the edge of the Botafogo beach, he looked at the moving cable cars on the Sugarloaf Mountain. One climbed up as the other went down with passengers. And although it seemed like he was going up, he knew his "cable car" was going down. And he could not see how he could interrupt its descent. He took Gisella's advice and started reading self-help books. Some of them even had a little useful content. Others began well, but by chapter three they went through a path of ideas that were not practical or that were quite questionable when it came to the purpose and meaning of life. Still, he had learned from his father and grandfather to be open, but critical, to new ideas. After all, no one held a monopoly on truth – if it that was a thing – and to better analyze an issue it was smart to listen to different ideas. That also meant he would raise an eyebrow whenever someone proclaimed themselves as guardians of the ultimate truth.

Whatever it was, the cable cars reminded him of a sentence from an author, an American guru, Alan Watts, that made no sense to him. He compared life to a dance, suggesting that there would not be an ultimate goal for life other than living it until its end. Just like we dance for the pleasure of dancing. No purpose, no expectations. It was an elegant idea, probably copied from some ancient philosopher like Nietzsche or Freud. And yet, there seemed to be something utopian or even devastating about thinking that a person can simply live for living, like an animal, without reasoning.

And what had he been doing if not that? Just like an animal, living day after day, after his father's death, with no purpose but to exist. He could not understand how this situation could be pictured as the meaning of life. Living for living.

Cheap self-help, that probably worked out fine for gurus or TV specialists. Real life was very different.

Anyways, he was already sitting comfortably and still had at least eight more hours of flight ahead. They had been flying for three hours already.

"Excuse me, I need to go to the bathroom."

Asked the passenger sitting next to him. He folded his tray table. The man seemed to be in his forties, like him. He stood up and went down the aisle. Felipe decided to stretch his legs, too, and did not sit down until the man returned, also because he was on the aisle seat due to his last-minute reservation. His right knee crackled when he stretched his leg and it reminded him of the inconveniences of age. He was mentally thanking his wife for the compression socks she bought him.

Suddenly, light turbulence rattled the plane, and some objects left in the seats fell. Among them were some of the objects that belonged to the passenger sitting next to him. Squeezed between the tiny space between the seats, he struggled to reach a laptop, a book and a handful of photos that had escaped from a small brown leather briefcase. He did not want to be nosy, so he quickly collected the photos. Snowy mountains, beautiful beaches, pyramids, a photo the man in front of the Statue of Liberty and finally a worn out photo, much of its color had faded, he saw a boy sitting in front of a gate, holding one bare foot and wearing a Flamengo T-shirt. He could not tell where it was. The place seemed strange. He hurried to put everything back in place before the man came back. He was not on the mood for conversations, especially when so many hours of flight were ahead of him. He was going to try sleeping if he could. As he put the photos inside the briefcase, he saw a book, he read the title: *Courage to Dream*. "Hmm, interesting."

"Thank you" said the man as he passed to take his seat.

"No problem. There was some turbulence. Did you feel it? Some things fell off your seat. I took everything I saw, but it's good to check if I didn't miss anything. I think I got it all."

"If I felt it? I almost peed all over the bathroom!" They laughed and Felipe's curiosity felt it would be a good time to contradict his previous decision of not starting any conversations.

"I saw the book you're reading. I read it too."

"Really? It's not very famous. Are you sure it's the book you read?"

He took the book from the man's hands, he opened to the first page: "How am I going to get out of here?"

"Yes, it is the same. That's him. Antonio da Silva" he confirmed returning the book.

"What did you think of it?" The man asked showing a discreet interest.

"If It's true, the story is very beautiful. He mixes philosophy and a little self-help. I'm from Rio and most of the story is set in Rio. I liked that a lot."

"I'm also born and raised in Rio."

"Nice. Well, that's a good read. I don't know if he wrote other books, but that one wasn't really for me" he concluded by sighing as he pointed to the book, now in the hands of its owner.
"Seriously?"
"It actually worked, but I didn't get the result I expected. The author talks about his difficult childhood and how he was driven to achieve his dreams. Somehow, the story touched me. And I thought if he'd made it, so could I."

He paused. *What was he doing? Ten minutes ago, he did not want to talk to anyone and just sleep; now there he was almost talking about his life with a complete stranger. A stranger wearing yellow colored socks.* He tried to get the flight attendant's attention.

"A whiskey, *on the rocks*, three rocks, please." He ordered as he thought "What the hell, what else do you have to lose?"

There is some truth when they say that you have nothing to fear if you have nothing to lose.

"Two, please" the man competed with a slight smile on the corner of his mouth, or was it an impression? The man put the laptop in the briefcase, and then accommodated everything carefully under the seat in front of him. Then he took the glass offered by the flight attendant.

"Cheers! Here's to important people."
"Cheers."
"And you, what did you think of the book?" Felipe wanted to know, clearing his throat after a sip.

The man reclined his seat a little, as if it were a couch, crossed his legs and turned the glass lightly to smell the whiskey. It was his second glass. Not that it was his favorite drink, but today he was drinking in memory of a great friend and mentor. What are the chances of sitting next to a reader? He laughed at himself. There was a scene that could go to a future book, who knew? The cabin lights had been reduced for the passengers' better visual comfort. The plane had pastel and blue tones that went from pale yellow to violet, almost purple. *What did he think of the book? What does an author think of his book?* He had written it for two reasons – so he believed. First because he felt he had a story to tell, even though he did not think it was anything phenomenal, mainly because his idea of success was quite different from what most people thought. Second because he had discovered many things about life and about himself and thought that the message of the book could be useful to someone. He had read many books, and even those he thought could add nothing to him had taught him some sort of lesson.

"I think it's a good story too. Unique, as we all are," he finally said after a sip.

"Yes… Each one of us has their cross to bear, it seems," he completed pulling a hair of his mustache while a mother accommodated her daughter with a blanket offered by the airline.
"But I think if I had been in his shoes, in that part of the job interview, I would have given up. He went on. His life was full of setbacks. Impressive."
"And that wasn't a third of what he went through, I imagine. You can't write about 40 years of life a few pages."
"That's true. He may have selected some events to tell the story" Felipe reflected as he observed the details on the yellow Christmas socks of the other man.
"As for not giving up, I think that as he had nothing to lose, so he had nothing to fear."

He was surprised that he had thought the same thing moments before that.

"Good for him." Felipe continued, loosening the collar button, and letting his body relax on the seat. "Still, his ideas didn't work for me. At the end of the book I decided that I would pursue the dream of transforming my grandfather's farm into a stud farm. Horses have always been my passion. My family has the financial resources and that wouldn't be a problem. My father was the obstacle tough. He was sure that I would follow in his footsteps, as he followed the footsteps of my grandfather's and of those who came before him and that I would continue the family business. He didn't accept my decision to set up the business. He did not understand that for me the stud farm was much more than a venture or a whim. It forced me to go further. The routine of the animals, the races, the new foals learning to trot."

"I perfectly understand what you mean by 'something that makes us go further'". The two letters embroidered in his shirt pocket said, F.C., probably his initials. He seemed to be in his mid-forties, maybe his late forties. He had turtle eyeglasses and a thick wedding ring on the left hand.

"And I was very happy. Everything was going well, except for our relationship, it was shaken and was never the same again. He said I was ungrateful to all to my family legacy and wealth amassed over the generations, for him I was a traitor to our family values. To him, I was a total and complete disappointment." Felipe, too, had nothing left to lose, he was talking to a stranger on a plane. He felt his voice fail as the tears came down, fortunately from the eye that the other man could not see. The memory of his father's death still hurt a lot, but he wanted to keep some dignity, he did not want to look more pathetic than he already did. He brought the glass to his mouth and felt the strong oak aroma in which the drink had certainly rested during the production process.

"And he died... while arguing with me over the phone about how he hated the idea of the damn stud farm!" He said. The words, once suffocated in his chest, reached his mouth, finally free to the air. "And now he is no longer here, and it is my fault; this dream has become a curse. It gave and took away purpose, it took away one of the people I loved most in this life. How could I know that happiness can so quickly turn into sadness and misery! And now I don't know what to do, how to keep going, how to start over."

Silence.

Some moments do not require words.

Antonio reached his shoulder and gently touched it in a gesture of sympathy.

"All our choices involve losses. And who likes losing?" He took a deep breath and neither him, nor Felipe knew where that tone was coming from "All my life, I made many choices and they all forced me to lose or give something up. My parents separated early, I'm not even sure they ever got married. And today, It's been exactly 10 years since the person who mentored me died." He added, also happy because the tear that fell was out of Felipe's sight. A few hours before, he was saying goodbye to his mother and sister, he was not sure he would ever see them again. Moving to a new country was an inconvenient reality, and being an immigrant, you cannot change it. On the other hand, in fact, we never know if the next farewell will be the final one or not. He continued: "The pain we feel is the only thing that truly humanizes, undresses and unites us." His attention was on the glass again, he used his finger to stir ice stones, they were almost dissolved. He recalled Paulo, his grandmother, mother, sister, Piquito – who had finally gained freedom a day when his mother left the window open. So many choices, so many losses... so many achievements... his apartment in Copacabana near the beach had given way to another, one of his own, in the Grajaú District, the same area where Paulo's old office used to be. Coincidence or and unconscious choice?

In the recent years he had seen more beauty than he ever thought would exist on earth. The gardens of Versailles, the Swiss Alps, the cold breeze of a spring morning on the edge of Lake Garda with his girlfriend at the time. So many colors, flavors, places. Now he was going to a new place, a new country. A new chapter written by his choices.

"Everything shall pass, my friend..." He said at last.

At that point, the combination of alcohol, cabin pressurization, low lights and the distant noise of the engines had worked on his traveling companion who had fallen asleep.

"Nothing like one day after another... and one night in the middle to get in the way."

#####

"Ladies and gentlemen, breakfast will be served in 15 minutes."

The announcement woke Felipe. Suspiciously, he opened his eyes, one after the other, it took a while to locate himself. Oh... The plane. Yes, Paris. The reality gradually came back to the executive's mind. He turned his head, his companion seemed to be asleep. He woke up rubbing his eyes and sat up straight. The conversation the night before had been so weird. He was talking to that stranger who seemed to know him so well. He, in turn, seemed familiar to him too. Not his face though. Besides feeling embarrassed, he felt good and relieved too. Talking to strangers! Why do we feel more comfortable confessing things to strangers than to those closest to us?

Breakfast was served, they greeted each other with a cordial good morning as if nothing had happened. However, he wanted to apologize to the stranger at the first opportunity. "*I was so inconvenient!*" He thought while putting a piece of bacon with grilled tomatoes in his mouth, part of the traditional English breakfast menu.

His travel companion immediately after eating, returned the tray and opened his laptop, he took the book and began typing something. He mumbled some words that were too low for Felipe's ears to understand. Something like... "and if" ... he could not hear. He gathered the courage he needed.

"I'm sorry for last night's sad conversation. I didn't mean to bother you."
"There's nothing to apologize for. It was actually very good for me. It's just that sometimes talking to strangers is really strange." They laughed at the wordplay.

"Passengers with connection to London must remain in the airplane. The others, please prepare for exiting the airplane."

The blue sky and a shy sun casted a golden light on Ireland's green coast below them, but as they approached the English capital, large clouds began to steal the sky as the plane went down, and the blue surrendered to the characteristic gray of that place.

"Where did my manners go? I'm Felipe Castro"
He said preparing for a friendly handshake.
"Antonio da Silva. Pleased to meet you."
Answered the other, shaking Felipe's hand.
"The author of the book?" He could not contain his astonishment.
"In person" Antonio smiled in confirmation.

Felipe was really embarrassed. How could he not have suspected it when he said there was a lot that had not been written? It had been a tip and he did not get it. What faux pas. And he said that Antonio's story, if true, was a good one, but it had not worked for him. Only that, the next day he realized it actually had. He had taken the courage to pursue his dream, but he had not succeeded. Or had he and just could not accept the implications of his choices? It was hard to tell. He would have to ask, even if he looked more ridiculous than he was already being. Maybe he knew something that might help him.

"All this time sitting next to you! I wanted to ask so many questions! You have also been an executive, as I am."

"I wonder," he laughed and continued, "I have no answers, my friend. Well, maybe the answers I have are not enough for you. I can say that some things make more sense to me now than before. But answers are very personal. I think we all have the potential to ask good questions, which, in my opinion, is much more important."

"Yes. You're right." He answered, a little disappointed though.

The conversation was interrupted by the pilot's landing procedures and maneuvers, the moment in which passengers usually focus on landing safely and soundly. When they were on the ground, the flight attendants began to open the plane doors. He politely asked to get up and pick up his suitcase that was in the luggage rack above them. Antonio was preparing a handshake to say goodbye to Felipe, who was faster:

"Sorry, but after everything we talked and the things you tell in your book, I need to ask: Did you win? Did you get there?"

Antonio placed the small carry-on bag on the floor, adjusting the brown briefcase in its side compartment. As he stood up, he looked Felipe in the eyes, who eagerly waited for an answer.

"I realized that I had 'won' a few years ago, when I looked back and realized everything I had done and gone through to live in a beautiful place, away from the favela, poverty and violence. I was walking through Grajaú and admiring the small marmosets that played on the electric wires of the poles and the shouting pionus parrots going from one tree to the other, the flamboyant trees that offered their flowers, the clean streets and the colorful houses, perfectly aligned. I saw myself surrounded by so much beauty that sunny morning that I finally understood it.

"What?"

"That it's never about winning, but about fighting and never giving up."

The End

www.dowslleyeditora.com.br

Este livro foi impresso no Rio de Janeiro, em novembro de 2020,
em papel Polén 80 gramas, com fonte Arial 12.